NEW INSIGHTS into BUSINESS

Trappe

Contents

Map of Student's Book

	Lead-in	Reading	Vocabulary development	*Language Focus*	*Skills Focus*
Unit 1 *Company Structures* *page 4*	**Listening** – The departments in a company Philips organisation chart	'The Philips Story' (*www.news.philips.com*) Company profile	Verbs and prepositions	Present perfect and past simple Describing changes	**Listening** – Describing responsibilities in a company: Pat Guerin, Guinness Ireland **Speaking** – Describing jobs; presenting companies **Writing** – A company profile
Unit 2 *Recruitment* *page 14*	**Reading** – Graduate career opportunities (*www.cognex.com*)	'Fit For Hiring? It's Mind Over Matter' (*New York Times*) Recruitment techniques Dictionary skills	Compound nouns	Present simple and present continuous	**Listening** – A job advertisement **Writing** – The CV and letter of application **Listening** – Selecting candidates and job interviews **Speaking** – Role-play of a job interview
Unit 3 *Retailing* *page 25*	**Listening** – Janet Moore, a retail specialist	'Richer Pickings' (*Business*) Profile of hi-fi chain Richer Sounds	Compound nouns	*Make* and *do* Locating objects	**Listening** – Store layout **Speaking** – A consumer survey **Writing** – A consumer survey report
Unit 4 *Franchising* *page 34*	**Listening** – A business adviser on franchising	'One day in my life' (*University of Warwick Network*) Profile of Vanessa Stein, a McDonald's franchisee	Suffixes	Adverbs *Used to do; be used to doing*	**Reading** – Bang & Olufsen franchise brochure **Listening** – Janis Errickson, a Dunkin' Donuts franchisee **Speaking** – Choosing a franchise **Writing** – An e-mail message: applying for franchise information
Unit 5 *International Business Styles* *page 44*	**Reading & Speaking** – Management styles in five different countries	'Learning to cope with corporate culture clashes' (*The Irish Independent*) The Centre for International Briefing	Prefixes	The imperative Adjectives of nationality	**Writing** – A memo **Listening** – Doing business in Japan: Tomomi Moriwake **Speaking** – Giving and asking for advice: cross-cultural consulting
			Review 1 *page 54*		
Unit 6 *Banking* *page 56*	**Listening** – Eleanor Stevens, branch manager with HSBC Bank Banking items and documents	'Picture the Scene' (*Bank of Scotland brochure*) HOBS Home and Office Banking	Abbreviations	*Allow, enable, let* First and second conditional	**Business Skills Focus: Negotiating** **Reading** – 'Are you a good negotiator?' **Listening** – Negotiating a bank loan **Role-play** – Negotiating a bank loan **Writing** – A short report
Unit 7 *Business and the Environment* *page 65*	**Speaking** – Environmental cartoons The role of business in environmental affairs	'Proven environmental commitment helps create committed customers' (*Marketing News*) Profile of clothing manufacturer Patagonia	Word building	Expressing contrast The passive	**Listening** – A Body Shop customer survey **Speaking** – Convincing a sponsor **Writing** – A letter of request
Unit 8 *The Stock Market* *page 74*	**Reading** – Headlines from the financial press **Listening** – Isobel Mendelson explains her investments	'Europeans Log On to Investment Fever' (*New York Times*) Internet share dealing	Phrasal verbs 1	The third conditional *Yet, still, already*	**Reading** – Analysing share price listings **Listening** – A radio stock market report **Speaking** – Buying shares **Writing** – A summary of a newspaper article

	Lead-in	Reading	Vocabulary development	*Language Focus*	*Skills Focus*
Unit 9 *Import Export* *page 84*	**Listening** – Why countries trade: an OECD economist **Reading & Speaking** – European Union quiz	'Profile: BARCO of Belgium' (*The Financial Times*) Breaking into new export markets	Compound adjectives 1	The future Describing trends	**Listening** – The invoice; descriptions of exports based on graphs **Reading** – The bill of lading **Writing** – Description of exports based on a graph **Speaking** – Completing a graph
Unit 10 *Company Performance* *page 96*	**Listening** – Departments of Pricewaterhouse Coopers	'Anatomy of an annual report' (*IBM Guide to Understanding Financials*) Description of the sections of an annual report	Nouns and prepositions	Fractions and percentages	**Business Skills Focus: Presentations** **Listening** – Financial analyst Carole Imbert talks about the pharmaceutical sector and gives a short presentation **Speaking** – Giving a presentation on L'Oréal **Writing** – A company report on L'Oréal
Review 2 *page 104*					
Unit 11 *Setting Up a Business* *page 106*	**Speaking** – Advantages and disadvantages of different types of company; checklist for starting a business	'The idea man' (*The Wall Street Journal Europe's Convergence*) Profile of Roger Foster, founder of Apricot	Prefixes	Relative clauses	**Speaking** – Questionnaire: 'How do you rate as an entrepreneur?' **Listening** – How the freight company Cargolifter started **Writing** – A business plan
Unit 12 *Corporate Alliances and Acquisitions* *page 116*	**Reading** – Extracts from the financial press **Listening** – Margareta Galfard on why the merger between Renault and Volvo failed	'When egos collide' (*The European*) Why mergers and acquisitions often fail	Phrasal verbs 2	Modal verbs of obligation	**Business Skills Focus: Meetings** **Listening** – A consultant gives advice about meetings **Speaking** – The language of meetings **Role-play** – A meeting **Writing** – Minutes of a meeting
Unit 13 *Marketing* *page 125*	**Listening** – Military metaphors **Speaking** – Market research techniques	'Hello to the good buys' (*www.shell.com*) A Shell Oil market research project	Compound adjectives 2	Comparison Reported speech	**Reading** – Direct mail marketing **Writing** – A direct mail marketing letter
Unit 14 *Product and Corporate Advertising* *page 134*	**Speaking** – Advertising media **Reading** – Advertising slogans **Speaking** – Controversial advertising	'Sacrilege' (*The European*) A controversial advertising campaign	Uses of *like*	Gerund and infinitive The article	**Listening** – A description of a Gillette TV commercial **Discussion** – Designing a TV commercial **Writing** – A scenario for a TV commercial **Speaking** – Presenting a scenario
Unit 15 *The Business Media* *page 144*	**Listening** – An executive describes Bloomberg business news services	'Profile: A Man And His Information Machine' (*New York Times*) Michael Bloomberg and his business media empire	Phrasal verbs 3	*could have* + past participle Nouns	**Listening** – A radio business news bulletin **Reading** – Business news articles **Speaking** – Preparing a radio business news bulletin **Writing** – Business news reports **Role-play** – A radio business news bulletin
Review 3 *page 152*					

Communication Activities page 154 Grammar Reference page 164 Word List page 172

Introduction

New Insights into Business, like the highly successful *Insights into Business*, is a comprehensive intermediate to upper-intermediate course for business students and practising professionals. It provides an authentic framework for developing an understanding of key areas of contemporary business, while allowing students to improve their language skills through a variety of relevant and challenging activities. To ensure authenticity, each unit has been prepared in close collaboration with major companies and institutions. The course meets the curriculum and syllabus requirements of business studies courses and is an ideal preparation for business examinations.

In addition to the popular elements of the previous edition, several new features have been introduced to the *New Insights into Business* Teacher's Book, Student's Book and Workbook to ensure an even more stimulating and communicative approach to learning business English.

Detailed information about these new features is at the end of this Introduction.

The Teacher's Book

Key vocabulary

This short introductory section familiarises students with the theme of the unit and provides explanations of core vocabulary. Key words are given with corresponding definitions or presented in such a way that their meanings can be easily deduced from the context.

The theme can be presented orally and you can ask students to contribute any relevant vocabulary that they may already have. Alternatively, and particularly for larger groups, ask students to study this section in advance. Draw attention to the words highlighted in the Key vocabulary section by, for example, writing them on the board. Check students' comprehension of these words before going any further into the unit. You may wish to give students the relevant photocopiable key vocabulary exercise available on pages 66–73, or you may prefer to use this towards the end of the unit to ensure that the most important vocabulary has been assimilated before moving on to the next unit.

Lead-in

The Lead-in section encourages students to reflect on the unit topic. It can take various forms, from listening exercises to speaking activities that involve either pair work or discussion. Invite students to contribute any relevant personal experience or knowledge they may already have. Details on how to exploit this material are provided within the Teacher's Book.

Reading

Each reading passage is taken from a British, Irish or American newspaper, business publication or company literature. While some of these texts provide an overview of the subject of the unit, others have been chosen because they present the people or issues involved from an individual perspective. The passages, which vary in length and degree of difficulty, can either be read in class or prepared beforehand. Check comprehension using the exercises that follow; including activities such as true/false, multiple choice and grid completion.

Vocabulary

Two or three vocabulary exercises follow the reading passage. The first one or two test students' comprehension of topic-related vocabulary items taken from the passage through a variety of tasks, including matching definitions, finding synonyms or antonyms, word building and crossword puzzles. The last exercise activates this vocabulary by providing a different context in which students can demonstrate that they are able to use the new words. Students are encouraged to use an English–English dictionary.

Discussion

All units provide activities to stimulate discussion, but some contain special discussion sections to encourage the class as a whole to express ideas and opinions related to the theme of the reading passage. In some units a series of questions acts as a stimulus, while in others students are asked to comment on documents, information or case studies.

Language Focus

New Insights into Business contains a standard syllabus of grammatical structures that intermediate and upper-intermediate students should already have mastered but which, in practice, often need to be revised. The Language Focus section deals with one or more of these structures and encourages students to consider these grammar points in a business context. The Practice section allows students to consolidate their knowledge. Comprehensive explanations of all these structures are given in the Grammar Reference section at the back of the Student's Book. Additional exercises in some units focus on certain problem areas of grammar which appeared in the earlier reading passage. All the examples are based on factual information taken from a variety of sources that will enhance students' knowledge of the general topic of the unit. The grammar exercises lend themselves well to use as homework assignments which can then be corrected in class.

Skills Focus

To develop the four skills of reading, writing, listening and speaking, each unit contains activities which set practical tasks and encourage students to provide creative solutions to authentic business problems. These enable students to consolidate and apply the knowledge they built up while working through the unit. In keeping with the overall philosophy of *New Insights into Business*, these activities incorporate authentic materials provided by professional organisations. Full instructions can be found under the relevant headings in each unit of the Teacher's Book.

Reading

Reading materials include fact files, case studies, promotional materials and questionnaires. These documents require detailed study as students will need to refer to them and exploit their content during the subsequent stages of the Skills Focus. When a document contains a potential problem area, the Teacher's Book includes a full explanation.

Writing

The writing tasks are designed mainly to introduce students to the most common forms of business correspondence (memos, letters, e-mails, reports, etc). Students are given the chance to express their personal views in other types of writing assignments.

Listening

In addition to the listening passages which may form part of a Lead-in, each unit includes a separate listening section where students will hear extracts from interviews, monologues and scripted dialogues. These interviews have been prepared with company representatives and other personnel specialising in each of the fifteen areas covered during the course. In this way, students have direct contact with business professionals who have invaluable insights based on personal experience and first-hand knowledge. The listening tasks have been devised to draw attention to this aspect rather than exploit only grammatical and lexical content. It should be noted that the majority of the interviews are authentic and were recorded with native and non-native speakers of English rather than actors. They therefore contain the hesitations, rephrasing and unconventional syntax which are a feature of natural speech. The dialogues provide practice in functional language and serve as models that students can use to prepare their speaking activities. The Teacher's Book gives clear guidance on how to use the listening materials, together with complete tapescripts.

Speaking

Speaking with confidence and using an appropriate style is essential to good business practice. Proficiency in spoken English is developed using different and often interrelated stages which combine role-play and small group discussions. The objectives of the role-play activities are to develop specific skills such as interviewing, making and replying to enquiries, asking for and giving advice, etc. Common expressions are suggested where appropriate. The small group discussions concentrate on providing students with a context in which they can express their own ideas more freely. Often a final speaking activity allows the class as a whole to compare and evaluate the work done in small groups.

Photocopiable material

Many sections in the Student's Book can be made more vivid and challenging by providing students with extra material, for example gap-filling exercises based on the key vocabulary, models for writing activities and additional background information for role-play and group work situations. You will find these materials on pages 66–99 and you are free to photocopy them. A key to the exercises can be found on pages 102 and 103. This photocopiable material includes:

- **Key vocabulary exercises**
- **Additional exercise for Unit 5**
- **Additional articles for Unit 15**
- **Business Skills** — Negotiations, Presentations, Meetings and Role-play exercises.
- **Writing Models** — Retailing Questionnaire Report, Letter asking for Sponsorship, Stock Market Articles and Summaries, Company Performance Report, Minutes and Direct Marketing Letter
- **Tests** — three tests to be used at strategic intervals in the course: a **Diagnostic Test** for needs analysis before starting the course, a **Mid-course Test** based on the first eight units and a **Final Test** to evaluate students' progress throughout the syllabus.

New Course Features

New Insights into Business is a completely revised and updated version of the popular *Insights into Business.* Like the previous edition the texts, listening material and activities reflect the latest developments in international business. In addition, *New Insights into Business* includes many new features:

Business themes

New units include: 'Company Performance' which explains key concepts in finance, 'The Business Media' which deals with the latest technological information sources available to businesspeople and 'Marketing' which features innovative approaches to this aspect of business. In addition, the original topics, such as Recruitment, Banking, Corporate Alliances and Advertising, have been reworked in order to reflect technological and information advances in the rapidly changing world of business.

Business skills

Interesting and interactive role-play exercises ensure that business skills are developed in an appealing and challenging way. They are based on the most important skills such as making presentations, negotiating, and chairing and participating effectively in meetings. New activities contain detailed instructions and background information enabling students to follow a step-by-step process leading from the language requirements to the actual practice situation. The authors have taken the organisational problems of large classes into consideration and designed the activities in such a way that groups or pairs of students can work autonomously while you give full attention to others.

Review spreads

Two-page vocabulary and grammar reviews follow every five units and are a useful and challenging addition to the Student's Book. They test students' progress before moving on to the next five business themes, using a wide variety of testing techniques.

Vocabulary development

In addition to the original vocabulary sections, each unit in *New Insights into Business* contains a Vocabulary development section which deals specifically with more problematic areas of vocabulary such as business collocations, phrasal verbs, business abbreviations or word building. This new feature introduces students to essential business vocabulary and encourages them to activate newly acquired language in a variety of tasks.

Extended language focus and grammar reference

The new edition provides a more comprehensive coverage of the types of structures that students at this level will find most useful. All practice materials present the language in a business context. An extensive Grammar Reference section at the back of the Student's Book includes additional information so that students can acquire more detailed explanations.

Dictionary skills

Because *New insights into Business* encourages students to develop autonomous learning skills, it offers comprehensive guidelines about how best to use an English–English dictionary and a business English dictionary. These sections feature sample entries from the *Longman Dictionary of Contemporary English* and the *New Longman Dictionary of Business English.* The entries are accompanied by full explanations of the different word forms, grammatical categories, spellings and pronunciation so that students can familiarise themselves with dictionary formats and gain confidence in using reference books outside of class.

The Workbook

The accompanying workbook has been designed so that each unit includes the following sections:

- **Review Spreads** — five spreads with test material as preparation for the following business examinations: LCCI, BEC and TOEIC
- **Reading** — a selection of texts from the media and professional sources on themes corresponding to the units in the Student's Book, together with accompanying comprehension questions
- **Vocabulary** — different types of exercises focusing on consolidating and developing the vocabulary of each subject area
- **Language Focus** — a selection of exercises reinforcing the various grammar points dealt with in the Student's Book
- **Writing** — a wide variety of tasks to practise standard business correspondence and writing
- **Listening** — a selection of interviews and dialogues featuring authentic recordings of business professionals

unit 1

Company Structures

Key vocabulary

Introduce the topic by asking students to present a typical company structure, writing their ideas on the board in the form of a chart. This could be a famous local company or one they have worked for. This will help students visualise the structure of a company and generate vocabulary they already know. Ask students to read through the Key vocabulary section and introduce the organisation chart, presenting the hierarchy from top to bottom, allowing students to comment on how it compares to their own diagram. Ensure that students understand the words in bold. You may wish to ask them to close their books and fill the gaps in the photocopiable vocabulary exercise on page 66 after listening to the cassette version.

Lead-in

1 Ask students to guess what responsibilities each person may have and then listen to check their answers. Play the tape more than once if necessary. You may wish to play again the extracts which caused particular difficulty, pointing out some of the vocabulary which might be unfamiliar to students such as *report*, *accountants* (speaker 1) and *design* (speaker 2).

TAPESCRIPT:

Speaker 1:
Every six months we produce a report showing how the company is doing. This past week, we've been busy with our accountants preparing the results that will be included in our next report.

Speaker 2:
I'm a member of a team of engineers and we've just finalised the design of our new portable computer. This model will be more powerful and more adaptable than our previous one. We're constantly looking for new ideas and experimenting with new products.

Speaker 3:
Before selling our latest product, our department must decide in which regions it will be the most successful and what types of consumers we want to reach.

Speaker 4:
Communication is a key aspect of my department's work. We answer enquiries made by our customers and are also in contact with the press to inform them of our new products and changes within the company.

Speaker 5:
We've been having problems with the quality of certain electronic parts made in our factories. So several members of the department have got together to talk about ways of improving some of our manufacturing techniques.

Speaker 6:
Our company is going through a difficult period and we have to reduce the number of employees in several departments and to review salaries throughout the organisation.

Speaker 7:
In today's changing work environment, computer systems play an essential role in how the company is run. In our department we not only ensure that all systems are working properly but we also design and develop new applications to make it easier for our employees to exchange and share information.

KEY:

1	e	Finance
2	g	Research and Development or R&D
3	a	Marketing
4	b	Public Relations or PR
5	f	Production
6	d	Personnel or Human Resources
7	c	Information Technology or IT

2 This task follows on from Lead-in 1 and is based on Philips, the company featured in the unit. Point out that the company organisation chart provided in the introduction to the unit is a standard one but that company structure and department titles can vary from company to company. Ask students what they know about Philips' products and if they own any. Then, working in pairs or small groups, students refer to the Philips Corporate organisation chart in order to decide which department or sector is responsible for each of the items in the box. Go round to each group, helping with any difficult vocabulary, for example *components*, *domestic appliances* and *computing products*.

KEY:

1 faxes
2 hairdryers
3 mobile computing products
4 lamps
5 X-ray equipment

Reading

1 Students work in pairs or individually to decide whether they think the statements are true or false. Encourage them to make guesses based on what they know already. Students then read the article as quickly as possible, focusing on global comprehension and finding the answers rather than concentrating on unknown vocabulary. You may wish to set a time limit. If you have access to the Internet, get students to look at the latest information and check that it is still true.
Website: www.news.philips.com

Students may have difficulties with the following:
Vocabulary: *diversification* (line 9) *creed* (line 47)
Idiomatic expression: *the turn of the century* (line 4)

KEY:

1 False	3 False	5 False
2 True	4 True	6 True

2 Emphasise that students only need to read the first section of the article again in order to find this information. You may wish to check students' pronunciation of years in English.

KEY:

a The company was founded in 1891.
b They established a new research laboratory to stimulate product inovation in 1914.
c In the 1920s, Philips took out its first patents and decided to diversify its product range.
d Philips launched the compact disc in 1983.
e Philips made its 100-millionth TV set in 1984.

3 This exercise provides an opportunity to work on numbers, often a problem area in English. Students only need to read the second section to find the answers. Once students have found the answers to the exercise they should practise reading the figures aloud in pairs, before listening to the cassette to check their pronunciation.

In English we do not make the words *hundred, thousand* or *million* plural when in a large number. For example, we never say '£4 *millions*', but '£4 *million*'.
Also with decimals, we say 4.32 as '*Four point three two*' not '*four comma thirty two*'. Point out that in English *and* separates the hundreds and the numbers which follow in GB English but not in US English:

12,839 = '*Twelve thousand eight hundred and thirty-nine.*'

452,210 = '*Four hundred and fifty-two thousand two hundred and ten.*'

6,391,000 = '*Six million three hundred and ninety-one thousand.*'

And is also used in numbers which contain no hundreds:

2,021 = '*Two thousand and twenty-one.*'

KEY/TAPESCRIPT:

1 two hundred and fifty-six thousand, four hundred
2 a hundred and fifty
3 six
4 three thousand
5 fifty million

4 This listening exercise provides practice in listening and understanding numbers. Play the tape through with short pauses for students to write down the numbers. You may want students to repeat the numbers for practice.

KEY/TAPESCRIPT:

1 7.4%	4 1,001	7 £6,391,150
2 364	5 13.57	8 0.2%
3 12,839	6 $451,210	

If further practice is needed, you could write some numbers on the board for students to repeat and/or students could each write eight numbers and dictate them in pairs.

Vocabulary

1 Encourage students to look at the words in context in order to deduce their meanings. Check students' pronunciation and show the stress on these words. Note the contrast between *innovation* (line 7) and *innovations* (line 8).

KEY:

2 h	4 e	6 c	8 g
3 f	5 b	7 a	

2 Students should first try this exercise without referring back to the text, as the first letter of each word has been provided. Point out that the number of spaces indicates the number of letters. To check their answers they should then scan the text to find the words which were actually used.

KEY:

2 concentrated on
3 programme ... expansion
4 launched
5 turn out
6 managed
7 monitors
8 implemented
9 divisions
10 issues ... practices

3 The purpose of this exercise is to activate and practise some of the vocabulary students have studied in Vocabulary 1 and 2.

KEY:

2 diversification
3 range
4 division
5 implements
6 monitors

Vocabulary development: verbs and prepositions

You could introduce this by asking students for any verb and preposition combinations they know or writing some verbs on the board and eliciting their prepositions. Then look at the examples with students.

1 Students should fill in the blanks provided for the prepositions and then check their answers with you or by looking them up in a dictionary.

KEY:

b from
c of
d in
e in
f to
g in
h to
i on
j to ... on

2 This exercise practises some of the verb and preposition combinations in context.

KEY:

b believe in	**d** depends on	**f** benefit from
c resulted in	**e** belong to	

3 and **4** These two questions could be discussed in groups or set for homework. Alternatively, students could write three gapped sentences for another pair to complete.

Language Focus

Present perfect and past simple

Focus students' attention on the sentences from the text and use the questions to form the basis of a class discussion on the differences between the present perfect and the past simple tenses. If you wish, students can refer to the Grammar Reference section on page 164 of the Student's Book.

KEY:

1 A – past simple
B – present perfect
2 present perfect (B)
3 past simple (A)

Practice

Before reading the article and completing the exercise, ask students what they know about Colgate-Palmolive. You could ask them to guess the age of the company, etc., and then read to check. Ask them to name products which are manufactured by the company. With a strong class you may wish to do this exercise first as a diagnostic test.

KEY:

2 did	**8** bought
3 began	**9** has had
4 led	**10** has maintained
5 has set up	**11** has created / created
6 has become	**12** has always paid
7 has developed	**13** has already made

Describing changes

This is a key business language point which students need to master early in a business course. There is more detailed coverage on pages 92 and 93 in Unit 9 of the Student's Book. You could start by putting arrows on the board and eliciting verbs and nouns for different types of change. Focus on the stress difference for nouns and verbs, for example, *'increase/in'crease.*

Practice

KEY:

2 rose	**5** fall	**8** rise
3 risen	**6** increase	
4 reduce	**7** go up	

Skills Focus

Listening

Introduce this task by asking students what they know about Guinness. Would they like to work for the company? What do they think Mr Guerin's job involves?

The pre-listening exercise provides students with an opportunity to focus on useful language and talk about personal work history. They may work in pairs or small groups to complete the task. You may wish to pre-teach the language by giving examples from your own history. Play the cassette for them to check their answers. Pre-teach *plant, Industrial Relations Manager* and *trade union* to avoid any comprehension problems.

Students already in employment could then be asked to describe their responsibilities and positions in their present jobs or in jobs they might have had in the past. Remind students that articles are used in English before jobs, for example *He is a journalist. I am the Marketing Director of IBM.* Point out that the gerund form is used after prepositions, for example *in charge of doing something, responsible for doing something.* Students could also describe part-time or temporary jobs they have done or what they imagine their future jobs will be like.

1 and **2** **KEY/TAPESCRIPT:**

When I first started working in Guinness [1]**I was employed as** a general worker. For three years [2]**I worked** in the bottling plant as a machine operator. [3]**The next position I held was** for a period of seven years in the engineering department as a maintenance assistant. This involved working with technically skilled personnel in maintaining plant and equipment. In both jobs [4]**I reported directly to** a supervisor. Since then, however, the structure of the company has significantly changed and the supervisor layer no longer exists. General workers now report to a plant manager. [5]**I was then promoted to** the position of laboratory officer in the quality assurance laboratory. [6]**This job involved** carrying out a wide range of analyses on all aspects of the brewing process. For the past year [7]**I've worked** in the personnel department as an Industrial Relations Manager. [8]**In this role** I report directly to the Personnel Manager of the company.

3 The purpose of this exercise is to train students to listen for general comprehension. Allow students time to read the questions and check they have understood them. They can then predict the answers. They may need to listen to the tape a few times to get enough information to answer the questions.

TAPESCRIPT:

My transition from general worker to a managerial position came about as a result of my involvement in industrial relations as an active trade union member for several years, as well as studies I undertook in my spare time. In fact I've recently completed a Masters in Business Studies at University College, Dublin.

While my current job title is 'Industrial Relations Manager', my role at present is more concerned with manpower planning. This involves talking with line managers to identify the manpower requirements of the company over the next three to four years. I'm also responsible for recruiting and drawing up contracts for temporary personnel as well as redeployment of permanent employees to new positions within the company. One of the consequences of major structural change like that which has taken place in Guinness is that job titles don't always reflect actual roles. In many respects Guinness is going through a period of transition where new roles are still evolving. If you were to ask me what, above all else, is the key competency for managers today, I would have to say it is the ability to manage change.

KEY:

1 He was an active trade union member and he completed an MBA in his spare time.
2 manpower planning and recruiting
3 talking to line managers and drawing up contracts
4 the ability to manage change

4 Here students may need to listen several times in order to provide a complete answer to the question.

TAPESCRIPT:

During the time I've been with Guinness the company has undergone several programmes of change involving the introduction of new technology and the contracting out of non-core activities such as security, catering and major maintenance projects. And this in turn has led to a significant reduction in the number of people directly employed by the company. I should add, however, that this was achieved without any industrial unrest. Guinness has always sought, has always sought to achieve major structural change through consultation and negotiation with trade unions. The age profile in the company was quite high and the necessary personnel reductions were achieved through early retirement rather than compulsory redundancies.

KEY:

The company has changed due to the introduction of new technology and the contracting out of non-core activities. In addition, there has been a significant reduction in the number of people directly employed by the company.

Speaking

1 This short role-play activity is designed to recycle language from Listening 1. It also provides an opportunity to revise the questions that are usually asked when introducing oneself at a meeting. As students prepare their list of questions, make sure that a wide variety of structures are being thought of in order to obtain information, such as *How old are you? How much money do you earn? What kind of company do you work for?* and *Where did you study?* instead of *What is your age? What is your salary? What is your company? What is your background?* etc. If necessary, you could revise question forms here. Students in work could do this about themselves.
Make a list of common errors and correct them after the exercise.

2 This is a similar activity, but focuses on company history rather than personal history. Each student should spend about ten minutes reading the profile of their company and should then ask their partner for the information needed in order to fill in the chart. As students work in pairs, make sure that they ask each other questions and exchange information rather than simply re-read the profiles. It may be useful to elicit additional structures that can be used to ask for information in the chart, such as *Where is the company based? Where are the company's headquarters? How many people does the company employ?* in addition to *How many people work for the company?* etc. Students in work could do this about their own company.

KEY:

Name of company	Virgin	Motorola
Headquarters	London	Chicago
Chairman	Richard Branson	C. Galvin
Business activities	cinema, hotels, communication, financial services, hotels, investments, retail and travel	advanced electronic systems, components and services, two-way radios, paging and data communications, automotive, defence and space electronics and computers
Main markets	the United States, the United Kingdom, Continental Europe, Australia and Japan	it conducts business on six continents
Sales in 1999	£3 billion	$30.2 billion

Writing

This activity can be done either in class, in pairs or small groups, or used as an individual homework assignment. If students have access to the Internet, they could also provide similar profiles of other companies by visiting their websites. Tell students that if they do not know the website address of a company they can try:

www.*the company name*.com

or: www.*the company name*.net

or: www.*the company name*.org

For a UK based company, they could also try:

www.*the company name*.co.uk

Or they could use search engines which are systems on the Internet that will search for any key word, such as 'Guinness'. Some of the main search engines are:

www.yahoo.com	www.Lycos.com
www.Infoseek.go.com	www.dogpile.com
www.GoTo.com	www.altavista.com

KEY:

Tesco is a company based in the UK since 1924. The Chairman is John Gardiner. The company's business activities include; superstores and hypermarkets, personal finance, e-commerce and an Internet service provider. Their main markets are the UK, Ireland, France, Czech Republic, Hungary, Poland, Slovakia, South Korea and Thailand. They also have plans for stores in Malaysia and Taiwan. Sales in 1999 were £18.5 billion.

unit 2

Recruitment

Key vocabulary

Bring 'Appointments' pages and sections from newspapers or magazines to the class. Brainstorm other headings and titles that are sometimes used in these such as 'job offers', 'situations vacant', etc. Ask students what they already know about the recruitment process and the different stages that are involved in getting a job in their country/countries. You may then want to read through the Key vocabulary section. There is a photocopiable gapped version of the recorded text on page 66. It is important to make sure that students have grasped the major differences that exist between British English and American English vocabulary in this field. You may also want to draw their attention to the many derivative forms of key words like *apply – application – applicant – application form, recruit – recruiter – recruitment* and *interview – interviewer – interviewee.*

Lead-in

1 This activity can be conducted either individually or in pairs. Check that students understand the vocabulary used and, as an introduction to the next activity, draw their attention to the style which is designed to make it as appealing as possible.

KEY:

1 Movie tickets ...
2 Tokens for pinball games ...
3 Plane tickets ...
4 President's Awards ...

2 This short section focuses attention on the personal qualities required for working at the company. It also encourages students to think about the best methods to evaluate whether or not candidates actually possess these. It is probably best to use this as input material which will contribute to the discussion phase at the end of the Lead-in. Avoid opening up the subject to classroom debate at this stage.

KEY:

Answers will depend on outcomes of discussions in pairs. There will probably be disagreement.

3 These are examples of recruitment techniques used in different parts of the world and illustrate how much recruitment processes can vary. They form a good starting point for group discussions as students' opinions will be very different. Before or after this discussion phase, ask students if they know of any other selection methods such as assessment centres, or any of the more marginal recruitment techniques that are sometimes used like morpho-psychology (which tries to determine personality from facial features), or astrology and numerology. By the end of the Lead-in, students should have a clear idea of what they think is an acceptable approach to recruiting personnel and they will then be able to contrast this with the views that are presented in the text that follows. If there is time, with a more advanced class it may be possible to ask students to actually perform the two tasks of telling a joke and making a five-minute presentation.

Reading

This text from the *New York Times* presents recent developments in the recruitment of business executives in the US, and shows how much more selective and demanding this has become through the use of testing. Students may have difficulties with the following idiomatic expressions:

mind over matter (title) *bring the wrong person on board* (line 45) *about as common as a ten-dollar bill* (line 74–75) *play the interview game* (line 76)

Ask students to read the statements first, then set them a time limit to read the text and complete the activity. You may want to ask them to justify their answers and perhaps correct the false statements.

KEY:

1 T   2 F   3 T   4 F   5 T

Dictionary skills

Being able to use an English–English dictionary is an important skill for learners. In particular, it vastly increases their autonomy. This section is devoted to developing reference skills by presenting students with sample entries to study. These are accompanied by a set of points to consider to help them to identify the various information that they can find about words and how they are used. The activity has been designed to provide a general introduction to dictionary use and as such it does go into a detailed analysis. You may therefore wish to extend this activity by introducing students to the phonetic alphabet or by providing their own selection of dictionary entries with accompanying texts. The two sample entries have been taken from the *New Longman Dictionary of Business English* and are typical of those in most English learners' dictionaries.

Dictionary checklist

KEY:

1 There is a difference between the pronunciation of the noun and verb forms. The former has the primary stress on the first syllable while the latter has it on the second.
2 The word can be used both as a noun and a verb
3 One meaning is given for each word form
4 No
5 No
6 The word is used as a verb (line 44).

Vocabulary

1 and **2** It is important to point out that it is not always necessary to go straight to the dictionary when you are faced with a word that you don't understand. Encourage students to first try to work out the meaning from the context; if that is not possible, they should at least try to identify the grammatical category that is used. In this exercise students are first asked to try to deduce as much as they can about five words by studying the context in which they appear in the text. Although they may be able to find answers to most of the questions in the checklist, they will need further information from a dictionary in order to complete others.

Being able to guess meaning is important for language learners and you may want to devote more time to developing this skill. They can do this by preparing their own texts and assigning a selection of words for small groups of students to work on. Each group tries to explain what they think the words mean and then checks the other's answers using a dictionary.

3 KEY:

2 position
3 employer
4 candidates/applicants
5 skills
6 behaviour
7 competent/suitable

Vocabulary development: compound nouns

This section deals with one of the ways in which compound nouns are formed. In this case the first element of the compound is a noun and the second one is a noun form with *er* which has been added to a verb stem. There are many examples of such words in English and many new terms that enter the language are generated in this way. It is important to point out that such compounds are usually spelt as two separate words, but can also be one word or hyphenated.

1 and 2 KEY:

1 **h** risk-taker
2 **e** computer programmer
3 **f** problem-solver
4 **b** award winner
5 **a** wage-earner
6 **g** wine importer
7 **c** law-breaker
8 **d** troubleshooter

3 There are hundreds of possible answers including; *trouble maker, law maker, pop singer, news presenter, record breaker, film maker, ski instructor.*

Discussion

This section simply provides students with an example of the questions found in a personality test of the type mentioned in the text.

Language Focus

Present simple and present continuous

This exercise reviews the different uses of the present simple and present continuous and allows students to revise the basic rules for these two tenses. You may want to refer students to the Grammar Reference material on page 164 of the Student's Book.

KEY:

2 **c** P. cont.
3 **a** P. simple
4 **d** P. cont.
5 **g** P. simple
6 **b** P. cont.
7 **e** P. simple

Practice

You may want to review the tenses when this activity has been completed, especially if it has been done for homework.

KEY:

2 feels
3 is not using
4 is looking for
5 realises
6 is growing
7 reads
8 is living
9 says
10 decide
11 travels
12 enjoys
13 is attending

Skills Focus

Listening

Before doing the Listening task it may be necessary to explain the meaning of certain words such as *mother tongue, glamor* and *gritty*. Encourage students to make notes during the first listening and not to try to complete the task at this stage.

TAPESCRIPT:

Fiona:
Hi, it's Fiona here. I just wanted to tell you that I saw this great job ad in the newspaper the other day.

Friend:
You never told me that you were thinking of getting a new job!

Fiona:
Well, I wasn't until I saw this one. It's exactly what I've always wanted to do.

Friend:
Go on then. Tell me about it.

Fiona:
Well, it's for a Californian company called Patagonia. I'm sure you've heard of them before.

Friend:
Oh yeah, they're the people who make outdoor clothing, right?

Fiona:
Exactly. Anyway they're looking for what they call a public affairs associate. It's basically a public relations position.
Friend:
Do they say what sort of a person they're looking for?
Fiona:
Well, actually the ad just says that they want someone who has experience in the press and in PR, and who has good writing skills. Oh, and it has to be someone who's pretty good at outdoor sports, you know, like skiing.
Friend:
Sounds just right for you. Don't tell me that if you get the job you'll be moving to America!
Fiona:
Oh no. I forgot to tell you, in fact they're looking for someone whose mother tongue is German, because the job is based in Munich, which would suit me just fine because, as you know, I've got family near there.
Friend:
Do you know how much the job pays?
Fiona:
No ... they don't say anything about money. But I'm going to apply anyway. I'm sure I'll find that out if I get as far as the interview.
Friend:
When will they be doing the interviews?
Fiona:
In the ad it says during the last week of February.

KEY:

1 Public Affairs	**5** German
2 Munich	**6** Californian
3 PR/press	**7** outdoor clothing
4 writing	**8** February

Preparation for writing

1 The curriculum vitae

This activity offers students an opportunity to study the layout and content of a curriculum vitae (CV) in English. Furthermore, it will allow students to prepare their own CVs for future use. It is important to explain that there are many different ways to prepare a CV, depending on the nationality of the company that you are applying to. For instance, in the US it is much more common to accompany each entry on a CV with a description of exactly what this involved, whereas in Europe a simple summary often suffices. Similarly, the order in which different events are presented may vary. The relative importance of extracurricular activities and of references will also vary with national culture. Much depends on methods of recruitment. For example, there is a current trend in using recruitment consultants, who invite prospective employees to e-mail CVs direct or advertise themselves on the Internet. In some fields, CVs have recently changed radically by abandoning the traditional chronological development through education and experience, in favour of setting out personal skills acquired in order to entice prospective employers. You may want to initiate a discussion on the merits of different approaches to preparing CVs.

KEY:

2 Education	**5** Activities
3 Professional Experience	**6** References
4 Skills	

2 The letter of application

This activity invites students to study the vocabulary and the style of a standard covering letter. As well as being a useful model for their personal future reference, it will help students to complete the writing task below.

KEY:

2 d	**5** e	**8** b
3 g	**6** a	**9** j
4 c	**7** h	**10** i

3 This section can be a discussion activity where pairs of students have the chance to express their views and then decide whether they think Fiona Scott is the right person for the job. Different opinions can then be shared with the class as a whole.

Writing

This activity provides students with an opportunity to practise writing their own CVs and letters of application. Encourage students to read the advertisement carefully and make sure that they have understood exactly what type of applicant is being sought. They can then work in pairs to prepare a suitable letter of application. You will need to help with the wording. They will need to accompany this with an appropriate CV. The CV can be prepared in groups or given out as a homework assignment. Remind them of issues related to the approach, content and wording of the CV.

Listening

1 TAPESCRIPT:

Personnel Manager:
The most important thing when interviewing a candidate is his character, his ability to react, his intelligence and his suitability for the position that ... which ... for which he is being interviewed.
Interviewer:
And uh, to what extent does the person's appearance influence your decision?

Personnel Manager:
It doesn't influence the decision, uh, but it does have some bearing on the decision, if you can take the difference between the two. It is important that the guy, the person, is well presented, is neat and tidy, and that he has a good manner, uh, because that shows a lot about his personality.

Interviewer:
Do you expect the candidate to be prepared in any way for the interview, or how should he prepare himself for the interview?

Personnel Manager:
Well, it's not a question of preparing himself. In the position in which I am, uh, normally the candidate's had at least one or maybe two interviews with other members, more junior member of staff before he gets to my level, unless the particular candidate is going to report to me, and in which case I expect the person concerned to have a fairly good knowledge of: (1) what the company does, (2) what he's going to be expected to do, and (3) who he's going to report to. Those things, those three items are very, very important and if the candidate, uh, does not give an impression of either understanding one of those three items, then obviously then he gets marked down accordingly.

Interviewer:
How does a candidate go wrong?

Personnel Manager:
The major way a candidate goes wrong is by basically becoming a yes-man or a yes-woman and agreeing with everything you say. What is most important ... One of the most important things about interviewing a candidate is the chemistry between somebody, between the two people in the interview, em, it's very very important – he has to have a spark, you have to feel as though that guy is going to contribute, that guy's going to be good and you're going to get something out of that person and he has to show himself to be not just 'Yes sir, thank you very much. Yes I agree with that, I agree with that.' Sometimes I lay dummy questions in which I want a 'no' answer and if he continues to say 'yes' then he goes down.

Interviewer:
What would your advice be to a candidate, er, going to an interview. How would you advise him?

Personnel Manager:
Uh, the first thing I would say to him is first of all to listen, secondly, to ask the right questions, and thirdly, perhaps the most important, is to create the right relationship which is, I guess, an adult-to-adult relationship with the interviewee or the interviewer. It is very important and that's what I said before is when you get a yes-man in front of you, or a yes-woman, then that person is obviously not creating an adult-to-adult conversation. He's creating an adult-to-child conversation and in most cases, managers are not, if they're good and they know what they want, they're not going to be interested in employing a child.

KEY:

1 b the qualities a candidate must have
2 d the kinds of things a candidate is expected to know
3 a the mistakes a candidate can make in an interview
4 c his advice to interviewees

Notes: (these are suggestions only)

Qualities: an ability to react quickly, be intelligent, be suitable for the position. The person should be well presented, pleasant and tidy.

Things he/she is expected to know: He/she should have fairly good knowledge of what the company does, what he/she is expected to do, who he/she is going to report to.

The mistakes a candidate can make in an interview: to say 'yes' and agree with everything the interviewer says.

His advice to interviewees: listen, ask the right questions, create a good relationship with the interviewer.

2 Invite students to predict the missing stages before they listen and complete the task.

TAPESCRIPT:

Personnel Manager:
The interview normally takes place by me being informed that the candidate has arrived, in which case, um, I leave my office and go and greet him in the reception area and bring him personally into my office and sit him across the desk, or across my office desk to me, and we proceed, uh, from there ... I normally start by asking the candidate to tell me what he ... since he's been probably through two or three other interviews previous ... what the job is that he's being expected to do, just to make sure that he's understands fully. Then I ask him to tell me a little bit about the company that we're working for, that I'm working for anyway, so that he's at least understood exactly what we do or the basics of what we do anyway ... er then I normally review his CV, and in particular either his previous employment or his current employment which is very important. Basically this is done to try to draw the candidate out, see how good he is at expressing himself, and to see what kind of character he is. Then I normally give him my views of what the position is that we're recruiting for and also my view about the company, then I normally give him a period of 5 to 10 minutes to ask some questions. Then I go back to him and just talk about him, and maybe then when he's fully relaxed, or more relaxed, put in a few of the trick questions, not a few, I would say usually normally one or maybe two maximum.

As I said in a previous question, it normally lasts a minimum of 45 minutes if the candidate is up to scratch and can go on for about an hour.

KEY:

1 The interviewer is informed that the candidate has arrived
2 *The interviewer greets the candidate and brings him into the office*
3 The candidate is asked what he/she knows about the job and the company
4 *The interviewer reviews the CV*
5 The interviewer gives the candidate his views on the job and the company
6 *The candidate asks questions for about 5 or 10 minutes*
7 *The interviewer asks more general questions about the candidate's life, and adds one or two trick questions at the end of the interview*

3 After completing this activity, you may want to brainstorm other expressions and questions which could be used during the different stages in 2 above.

KEY:

a 7	**c 3**	**e 7**	**g 7**
b 4	**d 2**	**f 4**	**h 6**

Speaking

This simulation exercise provides students with an opportunity to use vocabulary and structures they studied in this unit through a role-play of an actual interview situation. The activity involves quite detailed preparation so enough time should be allowed for this. Students divide into pairs.

The A students meet as a group to decide how they will conduct their interviews and what questions they will ask. They can use the flowchart from Listening 2 to help them. Check that they have well formulated questions corresponding to each of the sections that they wish to include. Encourage them to prepare one or two trick questions like *Can you tell me when you last lost your temper?*, *How do you deal with difficult people?* or *What is your biggest defect as a person?* etc. Students should try to anticipate the questions that the B students may ask about the job and the company.

The B students can use this time to familiarise themselves with key details in their CVs that they will need to emphasise. They will also need to anticipate the questions that they may be asked about their experience, education, skills, etc. Since some students may never have been interviewed for a job, you may need to help students to prepare a list of questions to ask their interviewer about the job and the company.

During the interviews check that Student A is using correctly formulated questions such as *I see here that you worked during the summer holidays at a summer camp. Could you tell me a little more about this?* and not questions like *What is your work experience?* It is also important that Student B does not simply read from the CV. You may want to invite students to observe each other's role-play and offer feedback.

unit 3

Retailing

Key vocabulary

This section provides a simplified description of the retail sector in the United Kingdom. This can be introduced by building up a diagram on the board to show the different types of outlets. You can ask students to give examples of each type from their own country. You may wish to give students additional retailing terminology and explain what is meant by such terms as *wholesale* (the sale of goods in large quantities to retailers and not to consumers), *co-operatives* (a retail organisation whose aim is not to make profits but to provide benefits to members) and *cash and carry* (a business that sells goods at discount on condition that buyers pay cash and carry the goods away themselves). Turn to page 67 for a photocopiable, gapped version of this activity and/or use the cassette version.

Lead-in

1 Students may want to make notes first in order to prepare. Encourage them to use the pictures for ideas. Various trends have emerged over the last few years in most countries such as the increase in the number of multiple retailers operating from large-scale outlets or the growth of electronic commerce (e-commerce) over the Internet.

2 Get students to discuss possible differences that they think may exist between UK and US retailing. Once they have looked at the logos ask them how many of these they recognise. Do they know what products each company sells?

In the interview, Janet Moore, who is a professor of retail studies, describes some of the reasons behind the success or failure of UK retailers to penetrate the US market.

Websites of companies:

Habitat: www.habitat/international.com

The Virgin Group: www.virgin.com

The Body Shop: www.bodyshop.co.uk

Next: www.next.co.uk

TAPESCRIPT:

Well, if you look at what has happened in recent years, it's fairly clear that, overall, British retailers have been unsuccessful in their efforts to sell into the US market. I mean there are, of course, exceptions and some retailers now have very profitable businesses – The Virgin Group is a good example of this. But there is also a long list of companies who have found the experience an expensive one and who have either been forced to withdraw from the US altogether, like Habitat and Next, or who have had to join up with American operations in order to stay in business, which is what was done, for instance, by The Body Shop.

KEY:

1 The Virgin Group
2 The Body Shop
3 Next, Habitat

3 Go through the list first and check that students understand any difficult vocabulary such as *assume, taste, invest, react*.

Students should be able to identify some of the more obvious sources of problems such as 1 and 2. Encourage them to explain their choices. Check their answers with the recording.

KEY:

1 yes ✓	4 no	7 no
2 yes ✓	5 yes ✓	8 yes ✓
3 no	6 no	

TAPESCRIPT:

I think that there are several reasons for this. One of the main ones has been that UK retailers don't seem to understand the basic differences that exist in the market and they tend to assume that just because people in both countries speak the same language they therefore share the same tastes and will like the same products. And that just isn't the case. I mean what can be perceived as traditional, high quality merchandise in the UK may in fact appear to be just old-fashioned and out of touch when it gets to the other side of the Atlantic. So that's definitely one thing.

Another difference lies in the whole structure of the industry and the way that outlets are organised. In the US, the market is dominated by the malls and so you really have to develop a presence there which, of course, means that if you're going to do that then you're going to need a big budget behind you. So maybe UK retailers have failed to grasp the size factor and haven't been able to adapt from a fairly small domestic market to the huge US one.

Underestimating the competition has also been another weak point. American retailers are aggressive players, their consumers are bargain hunters and the whole industry changes much more quickly than in the UK. So you've got to be well prepared to face your competitors and be ready to move quickly when you have to.

Lastly there is the problem of choosing the right places to open your stores. Some of the UK firms have done this by opening in the expensive town centre locations and then found out that they weren't selling enough to pay the rent! So, you know, I think it's really a combination of all of these things that has made it difficult for the UK companies.

Reading

1 As an introduction you may choose to write the name 'Richer Sounds' on the board and to ask students to guess what the two words imply about the company and the products that it sells.

Using the headline and the short introduction, students should be able to understand both that Richer Sounds has a unique approach to communicating with its customers and also that it has a unique selling strategy. Questions that they might ask could include:

How was the company started?

When was the company started?

What is it like to work at Richer Sounds?

How do they manage to sell so much per square foot?

What makes them different from the competition?

How many outlets do they operate?

What types of products do they sell?

You may want to draw attention to the play on words in the headline and explain that *rich pickings* means 'money or profits that you can get easily'.

2 Students should scan the text to find answers to as many of their questions as possible. If time allows, you could also review the questions that they were not able to find answers to.

3 Students should read the text in more detail. NB: the answers are in the same order as they appear in the text. Encourage students to justify their answers from the text. They may also have difficulties with the following:

Vocabulary: *niche* (line 53) *multiples* (line 56)
Idiomatic expressions: *raps out* (line 33)

KEY:

2 c (lines 8–12)
3 b (lines 60–67)
4 a (lines 71–78)
5 c (lines 81–82)
6 a (lines 98–102)

Vocabulary

1 This exercise aims to familiarise students with the idea of multi-function words (words which have two or more different grammatical forms but which have the same spelling). You may want to introduce this by putting a selection of words of this type on the board and asking students what these have in common. This might include such words as *contract, promise, switch, chair, profit, correct.* You can then ask students to add as many other words as they can find to this list. Other examples include *forecast, budget, record, report, control, supply, power, engineer.* You may also wish to point out that some of the two syllable words have noun/ adjective and verb forms which are pronounced differently. Examples: *contract, contrast, progress, perfect.*

KEY:

2 deal a noun
3 surplus b adjective
4 secure a verb
5 market a noun
6 model a noun
7 order a noun
8 control a noun

If you wish to extend this exercise you can point out that several collocations with *stock* are also used in the text:

stock turnover (line 47)

stock management (line 65)

stock control (line 68)

2 Sephora is a French chain of stores which specialises in selling perfumes.
Website: www.sephora.com

KEY:

2 stocks
3 deal
4 controls
5 secure
6 orders

3 Wal-Mart is one of the major American retailers which has recently started to expand into the European market.

Website: www.wal-mart.com

KEY:

2 f discount
3 b overheads
4 a profits
5 e suppliers
6 c niche

Vocabulary development: compound nouns

This section continues the focus on compound nouns introduced in Unit 2. To introduce this section, individual words can be put on the board, such as *service,* and students can then add other words that make up their compound forms such as *customer service, service sector.* Alternatively, you can ask students to find compound nouns in the text and then to add any others that they already know.

1 Point out that students' compounds could have either the first or second word added, for example *free market* or *market research.*

KEY: (suggested answers only)

a stock market, money market, market forces
b computer system, transport system, political system, banking system, alarm system
c brand name, household name
d special deal, special agent, special rate, special price, special effect

2 KEY:

2 f duty free	5 a purchasing power
3 d profit margin	6 b consumer goods
4 e sales figures	

Discussion

Allow time for students to read the extracts and to deal with vocabulary, for example *sort out, convertible, call of duty*.

In the case of Richer Sounds, quality customer service is a critical ingredient and staff are regularly visited by mystery shoppers who buy goods just as an ordinary shopper would, but then make a report about how the employee who served them behaved. You may wish to lead in to a discussion of the whole principle of incentive / bonus schemes like the Bentley Jaguar one.

The discussion should also provide an opportunity both for students to talk about personal experiences of good and bad customer service but also to say what they think of Richer Sounds' policy approach in this area. If students have visited other countries, they may be able to give examples of how customer service can vary from country to country. In this case, you will be able to get them to compare their experiences abroad with the way they are greeted and approached when shopping in their home country.

Language Focus

Make and *do*

Make and *do* create many problems for foreign learners of English as they are very often just one word in other languages. Although in many cases the expressions simply have to be learned, it may be useful to refer students to page 165 of the Grammar Reference material in the Student's Book.

Ask students to find examples of the two verbs from the text.

Practice

1 KEY:

Make **1, 4, 5, 6, 7, 8, 9, 12, 14**

Do **2, 3, 10, 11, 13, 15, 16**

2 KEY:

2 trip ... made	6 made ... suggestions
3 made ... complaint	7 money ... make
4 does ... good	8 plans ... made
5 do research	

3 Point out that some questions (e.g. 7) can be changed for individuals depending on whether they are working or studying.

Students can prepare two or three more questions to ask each other.

Locating objects

As an introduction, do a quick check of prepositions in the class, then focus on the pictures, asking *Where's X?*. Focus on *at* the top, *in* the middle, etc.

KEY:

2 on the right	9 next to
3 at the bottom	10 behind
4 in the middle	11 inside
5 on the left	12 above
6 at the back	13 between
7 at the front	14 in front of
8 below	

Skills Focus

Listening

1 This section starts with a short discussion to see how much students already know about the layout of supermarkets. You may want to use this opportunity to pre-teach some of the vocabulary that will be used on the cassette (*shelf, counter, aisle*, etc.).

KEY:

1 d	3 g	5 b	7 h
2 e	4 c	6 f	8 a

2 Students may like to listen again after checking answers.

TAPESCRIPT:

This store, like all our other ones, follows a standard design. For example, the main entrance is on the left because our research has shown that customers prefer to enter stores on the left and then they have a natural reflex to move to the right.

Fresh fruit and vegetables are always just inside the entrance. This is important because it gives a healthy image to the store.

The meat counter, however, is at the back of the store. There are two reasons for this, the first one being that meat requires a storage and preparation area. The other is that meat is an item that shoppers come to buy regularly and having it here means that they will see many other products on their way.

Likewise, basic products are rarely positioned next to each other. In this store, for instance, the coffee is in the first aisle, about half way down on the right, whereas the sugar is over in the fourth aisle nearest the checkout.

Breakfast cereal is in the second aisle, and you'll notice that the shelf at the top contains the lesser known brands. But the shelf just below it, which is at eye-level and generates the highest sales, is reserved for the more famous brands of cereals.

The four television screens that you can see above the demonstration area are showing various items that we are discounting at the moment. We have found that displaying products this way can increase sales of certain items by as much as 900%.

3 KEY:

- Customers prefer to enter on the left and then move naturally to the right.
- This gives customers a healthy impression of the store as soon as they enter.
- Since customers buy meat regularly, they have to go past many items before getting to the meat counter.
- In this way customers are brought into contact with many products as they shop for such basic items as coffee and sugar.
- Products placed at eye level sell best.
- TV promotion of products can increase sales.

As a possible follow-up, ask students if they agree or think that they are influenced by this.

Writing 1

The objective of this activity is to familiarise students with question forms and to give them practice in using these in the context of a questionnaire. You should assist students during the preparation stage by checking that questions are correctly phrased and coherent in the context of the survey itself. It may be necessary to give a more detailed explanation of the different question forms.

KEY:

a 3 b 1 c 2

Speaking

Emphasise that students must work with someone different. Make sure that students have had enough time to prepare their answers using the photos and give assistance with the input for this if necessary. It is important that they should have answers to all of the questions in the questionnaire and should have identified what products they actually bought in the shop.

Writing 2

While students will have limited data on which to base this report, this exercise should be used to help them to organise ideas and information for inclusion in a formal report. Explain that they will need to break up the report into at least five sections. You may wish to write up an outline of the structure of the report on the board, e.g.

Introduction:

Give the context for the survey, state its objectives and describe how it was conducted.

Section one:

Give information concerning the socio-economic backgrounds of the people interviewed.

Section two:

Show what services customers use, which ones they like/dislike and what improvements they would like to see.

Section three:

Describe customers' attitudes to using the Internet and direct mail to buy books. What proportion have already used these methods?

Conclusion:

Give the conclusions of the survey and summarise the main findings. Show which aspects of the business, if any, need to be changed and in what ways.

It is important that students are given as much help as possible with their reports. You may therefore want to put a list of guidelines on the board for them to follow. This could include:

- avoid using the personal pronouns 'I' or 'We'
- do not use contracted forms
- include linking expressions to provide contrast and establish sequences
- use both active and passive forms
- vary the use of tenses
- write a rough version and then review it
- use a dictionary to check your use of vocabulary

They may find it useful to consult the Grammar Reference sections on Reported Speech and Passive forms before starting the writing. You can also give students a copy of the photocopiable writing model of a report which you will find on page 74.

Franchising

Key vocabulary

Franchising is a relatively simple concept but there are some technical terms which students need to understand. As an introduction you can ask students to give the names of franchise operations that they know of and ask questions to elicit key vocabulary. Ensure that students understand the words in bold. You may wish to ask them to close their books and fill the gaps in the photocopiable vocabulary exercise on page 67 after listening to the cassette version.

Lead-in

1 Students should have no difficulty finding at least one example for each category as more and more international franchises expand into new markets. Some examples of typical franchises for each of these sectors include:

Fast Food: McDonald's, Dunkin' Donuts, Subway

Clothing: Benetton, Sock Shop, Accessorize

Motor Trade: Hertz, Budget, Rent-a-Car

You may want to ask pairs to work together and pool their ideas. In some cases you and students may not be sure if certain companies are actually franchise operations. In this case you can refer either to the website of the company or to that of one of the national or international franchise associations.

European Franchise Association: www.british-franchise.org.uk/effintro.html

British Franchise Association: www.british-franchise.org.uk

American Association of Franchisees and Dealers: www.aafad.org

2 This activity leads students to consider the implications and constraints of the relationship between the franchisee and the franchisor. Students should be able to think of some of the principal advantages for both parties but may have more difficulty identifying the disadvantages. It may be necessary to put some prompts on the board, such as *advertising, support* and *territories*.

Allow enough time for students to compare their lists before comparing their answers with another pair. Do not intervene if there is disagreement at this stage as this can be resolved after the next activity.

3 Again, encourage students to discuss this without giving 'the answer' which will come from the listening. You may need to check some words, such as *capital, expand, supplier* and *sources*.

Explain that students are going to hear a business adviser talking about franchising. Play the tape more than once if necessary, before checking answers. Some discussion might come from this.

KEY:

2 b	**5** b	**8** a
3 a / b	**6** a	**9** b
4 a	**7** a	

TAPESCRIPT:

Well, I think if we first look at things from the franchisee's point of view, imagine you are interested in going into business yourself. You have an idea, OK, but how can you be sure that it will work? Well in fact you can't. You just have to live with the risk that you, just like 50% of all new businesses, will fail. Now with franchising that's not the case because you're investing in a business that's already operating in other places. It's a safe bet. So that's the main advantage for the franchisee – reduced risk. But, of course, he or she has to accept certain conditions as part of the deal. For instance, there are rules that must be followed. This could concern perhaps where the franchisee buys his or her products from, what he or she can sell in his shop, the way the employees should dress and behave, the type of information that must be provided, such as regular reports on sales. However, in exchange it is true that the franchisee does have quick access if he or she needs advice about something.

From the franchisor's position it's really a very different view. The franchisor, the inventor of whatever the product or service is, wants to expand the business to cover as much territory as he can. Now the real advantage here is that he can do that without having to invest his own capital and without having to recruit and manage personnel. All that is taken care of by the franchisee. From then on, he or she can simply watch the increased fees coming in as his company expands. In addition to that, the franchisor can also keep tight control over the way that the individual franchisees actually manage their businesses and take action if things go wrong. Similarly if a franchisee wants to sell the business then they would have to get the approval of the franchisor. Normally the franchisor will also look after the business at national and international level which, of course, means promoting the business through national advertising.

Reading

You may wish to lead in to the reading by putting the 'golden arches' trademark on the board and elicit what it represents. Ask students what their feelings are about the company and what they think life might be like as a franchisee.

1 In this pre-reading section, students are being asked to classify the different types of work that a Fast Food franchise manager has to do. Go through the categories to check that students understand.

KEY: (suggested answers only)

- **a** recruitment, training, performance reviews
- **b** organising her own work schedule, allocating time for different tasks, prioritising
- **c** meeting other McDonald's managers, attending franchise conferences, meeting with the press
- **d** accounts, payroll, taxes, ordering supplies, advertising
- **e** waitressing, preparing food, taking orders, cleaning
- **f** doing anything that remains to be done – monthly accounts, balance sheets and planning future development

2 Students should scan the text quickly. Encourage them to look for the items on their list and not to read in too much detail. Check answers as a class and ask if anyone is surprised.

3 Students read the text in more detail. They may have difficulties with the following:
Vocabulary: *lasered away* (line 116) *cravings* (line 120)
Idiomatic expressions: *paid off* (line 41) *muck in* (lines 85–6)

KEY:

2 False (lines 15–20)
3 False (lines 22–26)
4 True (lines 34–36)
5 False (lines 37–40)
6 False (lines 57–59)
7 False (lines 89–93)
8 False (lines 97–99)
9 True (lines 100–102)

Vocabulary

1 Allow students to check their answers in pairs before going through them with the class. Make sure that students understand the difference between *records* and *report*. You may also want to check that they know whether two forms of words have different or similar stress patterns, such as:

re'cord (verb) 'record (noun)
re'port (verb) re'port (noun)
up'date (verb) 'update (noun)

KEY:

2 h **3** a **4** e **5** i **6** d **7** j **8** b **9** f **10** c

2 This is a practice exercise for the words in Vocabulary 1, and leads into an interesting discussion topic linked to the reading. You may also wish to check that students know where the main stress is in these words.

KEY:

2 re'port
3 up'date
4 'paperwork
5 'challenge
6 'maintenance
7 'records
8 'tackle

3 This short discussion activity serves to consolidate students' understanding of time management and of the related vocabulary. It may also provide a good opportunity to introduce other key terms from this such as *schedule* (verb and noun), *timetable* and *deadline*. You can give examples of how these words are used and point out the terms *on / behind / ahead of schedule* and refer to the collocation *to meet / miss a deadline*.

Vocabulary development: suffixes

1 This exercise presents some of the most common noun-forming suffixes, and introduces the question of changes in primary stress that may result in suffixed forms. You may want to give more examples of other suffixes and word forms.

KEY:

Same main stress as their stem:
as'sessment
ef'fectiveness

Different main stress as their stem:
'regular-regu'larity
ad'minister-admini'stration

Suffixes which do not cause stress to change include:
-er -ate -age -ite -ist -ism
-ish -y -able -ile -ate -ive

Suffixes which do cause stress to change include:
-ic -ical -ee -ese

2 Students can do this in pairs. If time is limited, give three words to each pair and then get feedback from the class.

KEY:

(stress changes are marked)

-ment	-ness	-ity	-ation
disagreement	willingness	confidenti'ality	organi'sation
requirement	carelessness	simi'larity	prepa'ration
investment	awareness	popu'larity	presen'tation

3 If students have difficulty finding other examples of suffixed nouns, give some clues, such as *When two people have the same opinion, they come to an .... (agree)*. Several more examples are given below:

-ment	-ness	-ity	-ation
arrangement	lateness	complexity	confirmation
management	effectiveness	liability	reservation

As an alternative, students can quiz each other – one pair gives a stem, the other says the corresponding noun.

Language Focus

Adverbs

This section provides a review of some of the most common adverbs used to situate the timing of events. Although most students will already be familiar with most of these, in some cases they may find it difficult to use the words correctly. This is often because of interference from 'false friends' which are words that have a similar form in English and another language, but have different meanings, such as:

èventuellement (French) and *eventuell* (German) = *possibly* in English.

eventually in English = *finalement* (French) and *schlieblich* (German).

actuellement (French), *aktuell* (German) and *actualmente* (Spanish) = *currently* in English.

actually in English = *en fait* (French), *tatsßchlich* (German) and *de hecho* (Spanish).

Before looking at this, students could underline the time adverbs in the text.

If the exercise proves difficult, get the students to do the ones they are more confident about, then discuss the others together. You can also write up four sentences about yourself as an example and leave gaps for the students to supply the correct adverb. You may want to refer students to the Grammar Reference material on page 165 of the Student's Book.

KEY:

2 eventually
3 already
4 currently
5 sometimes
6 usually
7 always

Used to do; be used to doing

As these two verbs are very similar in form but very different in meaning, students often confuse them or use them incorrectly saying *I am used to travel by train* instead of *I am used to travelling by train*. This exercise is designed to illustrate the differences between the two forms and to give practice in using them correctly. Again, you may want to refer students to the Grammar Reference material on page 166 of the Student's Book.

KEY:

used to + infinitive is used for things that happened regularly or for a long time in the past but which no longer happen.

be used to + -ing is used when talking about something which is familiar and no longer strange.

Practice

1 Students could try this exercise without referring to the text and then check any sentences that they are not sure of.

KEY:

b is used to helping
c is used to chatting
d is used to attending
e used to snore
f used to work
g used to have
h is used to taking

2 This writing exercise allows students to practise the language of time management and the two grammar points. Advise students to start with a description of what their lives are like today before comparing this with what they used to do in the past. You may prefer to give this as an expanded writing assignment, possibly for homework.

Skills Focus

Reading

1 Most students of Business English find that a Business English dictionary is an extremely useful tool. This exercise is designed to give them an introduction to the types of entries that are specific to such dictionaries. In this case, the extracts have been taken from the *New Longman Dictionary of Business English.*

Students do the exercise in pairs. If they have a Business English dictionary, they could use it to check.

KEY:

1 e **2** g **3** a **4** f **5** c **6** d **7** b

2 The sample entries give complete definitions for the words as they are used in the context of a brochure from Bang & Olufsen, the Danish manufacturer of television and audio equipment (Website address: www.bang-olufsen.com). You could write the words on the board and elicit definitions. It may be useful to go over the definitions with the class and to point to some of the problems that students may encounter, for instance, a number of other abbreviated forms are also used, such as *esp.* (especially), *i.e.* (id est – to refer to an example, often read as 'that is') and *usu.* (usually).

The text is an authentic extract from a franchise brochure, which has not been edited, and shows the level of difficulty that texts of this type may present. Depending on whether dictionaries are available for use in class, it may be necessary to ask students to consult them to find the meanings of other words that may present problems. The class can be divided into groups and several words can be assigned to each group from the following list:

display	public relations	know-how
shopfitting	legal	reclaimable
contractors	lease	funding
allowance	expenses	clearing banks
induction	leasing right	reward
direct marketing	right	

Groups can then 'teach' each other, either by re-grouping or as a class, before going on to complete the brochure information.

KEY:

2 fixtures and fittings
3 market research
4 charges
5 trademark
6 return
7 Gross Margin

Listening

1 In the UK, *doughnuts* and in the US, *donuts* – ask students if they know what these are and if they know the Dunkin' Donuts franchise, explain *dunk* (i.e. usually biscuits or basketballs). The interview provides an opportunity for students to hear an American woman talking about being a Dunkin' Donuts franchisee. Explain that the logos are all part of Dunkin' Donuts' parent company. Go through the chart, eliciting what kind of information goes in each gap and explaining that the numbers give the order of the information. Play the tape more than once if necessary.

TAPESCRIPT:

Well, the company that I am a franchisee with is called Dunkin' Donuts which has its headquarters in Massachusetts, here in the US. Dunkin' Donuts is basically a chain of bakery goods and we sell bagels, muffins, donuts, although the majority of our sales, in fact our most profitable item, is coffee even though we are a bakery. Dunkin' started in business way back in 1950 and opened their first franchised store five years later in 1955.

Allied Domecq is actually the central owner of Dunkin' and they also have other franchised businesses as part of the group. For instance, they own Baskin Robbins which opened in 1950, becoming a franchise operation right from the start. They're specialised in selling ice cream and also beverages, like sodas and shakes.

Togo's is also part of Allied and they're the youngest of the franchise brands since they only got going in 1971 and only really developed into a franchise operation in 1977. They what we would call a speciality sandwich chain. Of all three businesses, Togo's and Baskin's have the lowest capital requirements which are about $100,000 compared to Dunkin's which is double that.

KEY:

1 bakery goods, bagels, muffins, donuts and coffee
2 1955
3 $200,000
4 Allied Domecq
5 Baskin Robbins
6 ice cream, beverages, sodas and shakes.
7 $100,000
8 Togo's
9 1977

2 Janis Errickson now goes on to talk about the 'ingredients' for success. Students have a different kind of task to complete. Check that they understand the five topics, and encourage them to write key words.

TAPESCRIPT:

Well, I suppose that to be a successful franchisee you need a lot of dedication – a lot of dedication to the job. I think I would say that preparation is the most important part of that because in this business you always need to be looking at the future of even the day, the week, the month. That's probably eighty percent of the job in my view.

On the management side, I think the main thing is really to look after your employees because one of the main problems with the job is staffing, finding the right people to work with you. Let's face it. It's not a high-paying job so your staff have to feel that they are getting something else from working with you because if they don't enjoy doing their work then customers are not going to enjoy being with them.

It's never easy to handle the money management of the business since there's a basic instability in the whole thing. You can never be sure of exactly how much you are going to sell – it's unpredictable. You just can't guarantee that X number of people will come in and buy your product. But on the other hand you can be pretty sure that your bills will remain pretty constant so you need to be sure that you are constantly matching the two issues.

I think that you really have to be someone who has a certain vision. I mean long term vision, because when you start out you have to understand that you're not going to get rich tomorrow. The franchise business doesn't give you an immediate payback. So you have to be patient and enjoy the daily success of the business in order to maintain it.

Well, faith is certainly something that is very central to your relationship with your franchisor as they have certain standards that they want you to adhere to. You know, there are all kinds of rules that you have to respect so that there is continuity in the chain and you have to comply with them. So you must have confidence in the way that the whole business is being managed higher up because you are going to have to follow their formulas and that's easier if you can trust them and believe what they are saying.

KEY:

1 You always need to be looking at the future.
2 The main thing is really to look after your employees because one of the main problems with the job is staffing.
3 You can never be sure of exactly how much you are going to sell – you can be pretty sure that your bills will remain pretty constant so you need to be sure that you are constantly matching the two issues.
4 You have to understand that you're not going to get rich tomorrow. The franchise business doesn't give you an immediate payback.
5 You must have confidence in the way that the whole business is being managed higher up because you are going to have to follow their formulas and that's easier if you can trust them and believe what they are saying.

Speaking

This information gap activity allows students to learn about two unusual franchises and then to say what they think about the opportunities that they offer. Make sure that they have time to read and digest the information and check vocabulary. Encourage them not to just 'read out' the information, and make sure that they take notes.

Writing

1 Writing e-mails has become an everyday part of business life. This exercise familiarises students with a standard e-mail format and shows them an example of how such messages are written.

You may wish to conduct a brief discussion, asking students a few questions, such as:

Which students e-mail?

Does any student write e-mails in English?

Do students like using this form of communication?

If so, why? If not, why not?

KEY:

2 g	4 d	6 a	8 b
3 e	5 i	7 f	9 c

2 KEY:

1 Mad Science
2 science education and entertainment for children
3 1994
4 $55–60,000
5 8% royalty p.a.
6 franchise@madscience.org

1 Expense Reduction Analysts International Ltd
2 Cost management consulting
3 1994
4 £18,900
5 £100 per month in year 1, £300 in year 2 and £400 in year 3
6 info@expense-reduction.net

unit 5

International Business Styles

Key vocabulary

This section introduces the idea of the distribution of power in a business organisation and prepares students for the exercise that follows. Check that students understand the vocabulary in bold. You may wish to ask them to close their books and fill the gaps in the photocopiable vocabulary exercise on page 68 after listening to the cassette version.

Lead-in

1 This activity can be done in pairs or small groups. Using their general knowledge of Germany, Poland, Sweden, the United Kingdom and the United States, students should be able to identify which profile corresponds to each country. Lead into this exercise by asking what students feel to be the characteristics of each of these countries. Sometimes asking them to give the stereotype for each of the countries helps them to realise that they do have some general opinions about different nationalities. Even national stereotypes may help them to identify which management styles we may expect to find in a particular country. In any case, the purpose of this task is not to get the right answer but to gain some insight into cross-cultural issues in business as well as learning some new vocabulary.

KEY:

1 Germany
2 the United Kingdom
3 Sweden
4 the United States
5 Poland

2 Encourage students to consider the pros and cons of working in the various business cultures. Ask them to consider the problems they might have in adapting to different cultures. If students are from one of the countries, ask whether they think the description is true. Or they could go on to create a profile of a manager from their country, if it is not already given.

Alternatively, you can use the photocopiable lesson material on page 75 to organise group discussions.

Reading

1 The text deals with some of the differences that exist between business cultures. It presents 'The Centre for International Briefing' which specialises in training businesspeople to cope with culture clashes while working abroad. Students may have difficulties with the following:

Vocabulary: *minefield* (para 1)

Idiomatic expression: *tiptoeing through the minefield* (subtitle)

Reading 1 focuses on sequencing. Point out words to look for in order to find the correct answers, for example 'he' in **a**, 'it' in **b**, and 'such pitfalls' in **d**.

KEY:

3 b	**5** c	**7** a
4 f	**6** e	

2 Encourage students to explain in as much detail as possible social etiquette in their own countries. Some students may have amusing stories to tell, especially regarding British or American etiquette.

Vocabulary

1 Check students' pronunciation and understanding of the difference between, for example, *minefield* and *pitfall*, *custom* and *etiquette*. Students should give an example of each one in their country.

KEY:

2 g	**4** a	**6** j	**8** f	**10** b
3 i	**5** h	**7** e	**9** d	

2 This exercise practises words from Vocabulary 1 and gives further insights into cross-cultural issues. Ask students if they know any rules about gift giving in their country.

KEY:

2 abroad
3 etiquette
4 offensive
5 is a sign of
6 sensitive
7 minefield

Vocabulary development: prefixes

1 You could introduce this by writing 'im' on the board and eliciting words that have this prefix, etc.

KEY:

b dis-	**d** il-	**f** ir-
c un-	**e** in-	

In lists **a**, **d** and **f**, the words begin with the same letter.

Note: 'il' goes with **l**, 'im' with **p** or **b** and 'ir' with **r**, but words beginning with **r** do not necessarily always take 'ir'.

2 Students may use a dictionary if necessary.

KEY:

b dis-	**d** ir-	**f** in-	**h** dis-	**j** il-	**l** un-
c im-	**e** il-	**g** un-	**i** ir-	**k** im-	

3 Students could work in pairs to come up with examples of other adjectives, such as *disorganised, illegitimate, impatient, incomplete, unbelievable*.

Language Focus

The imperative

The basic form of the imperative is not difficult but students often do not know the emphatic forms *always/never*, etc. Check students understand *expect*, *assume* and *judge*. You may want to refer students to the Grammar Reference material on page 166 of the Student's Book.

Practice

KEY:

2 Don't judge
3 Invest / Do invest
4 Increase / Do increase
5 Study / Do study
6 Expect / Do expect
7 Don't expect
8 Be flexible / Do be flexible
9 Don't assume
10 Beware / Do beware

Adjectives of nationality

Students could underline all of these in the text on page 46 of the Student's Book and say if they are countries, nationalities or a person.

Practice

KEY:

1 Hola is a Spanish weekly magazine.
2 Ferrari is an Italian car manufacturer.
3 Evian is a French mineral water.
4 Mateus Rosé is a Portuguese wine.
5 IBM is an American computer company.
6 AGFA is a German photographic company.
7 Philips is a Dutch electronics company.
8 Carlsberg is a Danish beer.
9 IKEA is a Swedish furniture retailer.
10 BBC1 is a British television channel.
11 Olympic is a Greek airline.
12 Pravda is a Russian newspaper.
13 Aker AS is a Norwegian industrial company.
14 Istanbul is a Turkish seaport.
15 Nokia is a Finnish mobile phone company.

Skills Focus

Writing

A memo

Memos are similar to e-mail messages. Ask students if they have ever used e-mail. In what context? In English? Then go through the introduction with them.

KEY:

1 **c** When the memo is sent.
2 **e** Name of the person to whom the memo is sent.
3 **b** A short heading which tells you what the memo is about.
4 **f** A brief introduction to the memo giving the most important information.
5 **a** The 'body' of the memo.
6 **d** Conclusion, which often recommends a course of action.

Unlike letters, a memo does not contain forms of address (such as *Dear Mrs X*) or the sender's signature. The sender usually puts his or her name or initials at the end of the memo.

Listening

Ask students to think about Japan, and see if they can guess what might be said under each heading. Although the speaker has a distinct Japanese accent, she does speak slowly and clearly. Stop the cassette briefly at the points given in the tapescript so that students can organise their notes.

TAPESCRIPT:

I'm very glad to see you are interested in learning more about Japan, because you will never be able to do business in Japan unless you understand some basic … basic aspects of Japanese management and Japanese corporate culture in general.

In my seminars, I usually talk about three fundamental principles of Japanese management. The first is the emphasis on the group in Japanese corporations. The second is the importance of human interpersonal relationships. And the last point I discuss is the role of Japanese managers as generalists and facilitators.

All right then, we'll talk about, briefly, these three principles. The first point then, the emphasis on the group. This group orientation manifests itself in the following example (you can yourself conduct this experiment). If you ask any Japanese businessman what he does, he will almost invariably answer by saying, 'I am a Sony man', or 'I work for Mitsubishi', or 'I'm with such and such company', instead of telling you, if he's a, whether he's an engineer or an accountant, for instance, you see.

This point, this emphasis on the group, the group orientation explains the other two principles as well. For instance, Japan is geographically an island. It's an island nation, it's like a boat with an overcrowded homogeneous population. So this explains partially already why this group orientation is so important and also necessary for the very survival of Japan and Japanese corporations as well. You see, by the way, the people are the only resource Japan possesses. It is an island nation without any other natural resources. So it's the question of survival also.

Short pause here

That leads us to the second question, the second emphasis rather, namely the emphasis on human or interpersonal factors or relationships. In this overcrowded island nation, in order to achieve or survive together, they have to learn, like I said, to get along, and in order to achieve this, there are certain things they have to learn, like harmony. How do you achieve harmony? By, by er sacrificing a little bit of self-interest for the sake of the group. And also by compromising, by trying to have everybody agree, namely, to achieve or to arrive at the consensus of the group. You see.

Once you are employed, or hired by a company, you remain with this company until your retirement, the so-called 'lifetime employment'. That explains a lot of things already, like seniority order, because you enter the company along with your peers, the same age group. You graduated from the university together, so you get promoted together, and so you climb this company, organisational ladder, little by little together, slowly but steadily.

Short pause here

The last and third point or principle is a view of managers or executives as generalists and facilitators, rather than decision-makers.

In general, in a Japanese corporation, everybody is more or less trained to be a generalist rather than a specialist. So even if you are an engineer, when you have just joined the company, you will have this orientation and you will be transferred from one department to the other and you'll be rotated in every department of the company to familiarise yourself with the entire company and for instance, since you are not narrowly specialising in one field, you can take over somebody else's role.

I also talk about 'ringisho' the so-called 'ringisho' usually translated as 'the management by consensus'. That means that all the employees participate in the process of decision-making. They form small groups in each department and they discuss the matter with each other. They arrive at an agreement, the consensus, and then the departmental chief or the executive will have to agree himself or herself.

And this way, the consensus is achieved. Everybody is involved in the process. It's not like, say, an American way of decision-making by one big executive or the president.

This is just a brief description of my seminars, but I think if you attend them, I can give you even more insight into Japanese corporate culture, which I think will help you greatly in your coming business trip to Japan.

KEY:

Emphasis on the group	Human relationships	Japanese managers
The emphasis on the group is very important in Japanese corporations (i.e. a person will tell you the company he works for instead of the job he does). Also, as an island nation without natural resources, people must learn to get along with each other. This is necessary for the survival of Japanese corporations.	To achieve harmony, people make sacrifices for the sake of the group and try to agree with each other. Lifetime employment is also common. Employees of the same age who are hired together also get promoted together until retirement.	In Japanese corporations everyone is trained to be a generalist and can therefore take over several different duties. Management by consensus is also common. Decisions are made by all employees and not just by one top executive.

Writing

Remind students of the rules of memo writing, and make sure they answer the questions. They could perhaps formulate a plan in class and write the memo as a homework assignment.

KEY: (suggested answers only)

DATE 11th June
TO Philip Groves, Managing Director
FROM Vincent Mills, Human Resources Manager
SUBJECT Seminars on Japanese culture and management

I met Ms Moriwake, the Japanese consultant, who summarised the three main themes of her seminars.

1 The emphasis on the group is very important in Japanese corporations (i.e. a person will tell you the company he works for instead of the job he does). Also, as an island nation without natural resources, people must learn to get along with each other. This is necessary for the survival of Japanese corporations.

2 Human relationships are also discussed in the seminars. To achieve harmony, people make sacrifices for the sake of the group and try to agree with each other. Lifetime employment is also common. Employees of the same age who are hired together also get promoted together until retirement.

3 Finally, in Japanese corporations everyone is trained to be a generalist and can therefore take over several different duties. Management by consensus is also common. Decisions are made by all employees and not just by one top executive.

I've contacted everyone involved and any morning of the week starting the 6th of July would suit. Ms Moriwake, could start at eight in the morning and work through till twelve (with a coffee break). She could lunch with the participants allowing informal chatting about Japanese culture over lunch. I believe our executives should attend these seminars. A better understanding of Japanese culture and management will certainly help them in the negotiations in Japan. Ms Moriwake has agreed to our terms and is expecting you to confirm with her this week.

VM

Role-play

Giving and asking for advice

This activity will provide students with an opportunity to practise giving and asking for advice based on the themes studied throughout the unit. The activity involves both Students A and B in detailed preparation and sufficient time should be allowed for this. The A Students should use this time to prepare all the information they know about the country chosen (their own country or one they know well). They should go through the instructions provided, point by point writing down the advice that they will give to B Students. They may wish to refer back to the Lead-in section for some information, and you should provide help concerning vocabulary when needed, or, if available, encourage them to use a dictionary. The B Students should use this time to prepare a list of questions to ask the A Students. Check that students are preparing properly formulated questions about specific situations, like those provided for them in the examples and not questions like *What about the use of language?* or *Tell me about non-verbal communication.*

During the actual role-play, go around the classroom checking that students are using the language structures provided in the examples correctly. You could note down errors for later correction. For example:

Student B – *How important is it to be on time for business meetings in your country?*

Student A – *I would advise you to be always on time for meetings as it is considered very unprofessional to arrive late.*

You could round this off by asking each pair to point out something new they found out, followed by some correction.

Review 1 Key

Grammar check

1

2 have been
3 left
4 already
5 completed
6 graduated
7 Britain
8 joined
9 moved
10 include
11 means
12 currently
13 involves
14 used to doing
15 is expanding
16 are developing
17 used to think
18 always
19 intend
20 has agreed

2

2 Credit cards can be used at the checkout.
3 The company was founded in Germany and is still faithful to its German origins.
4 Have you received the letter I sent about the mistake your company made?
5 I'm not very tall, so it's difficult to reach items at the top in the supermarket.
6 What did you like most about the last job you did?
7 The position of Marketing Director is above that of sales assistant.
8 The Finnish company Nokia is one of the leaders in the mobile phone sector.
9 A well-written covering letter can make the difference between a successful and unsuccessful application.
10 The Irish President announced her intention to encourage foreign investment.

3

2 There has been a **drop** / **decline** in car production.
3 The price of this product has been **reduced**.
4 There has been a **rise** in the number of employees.
5 Orders **fell** this year.
6 The company has **increased** investment in new equipment.
7 The number of franchisees has **gone up** / **risen**.
8 There has been a **reduction** in the budget.
9 Franchise fees have **risen** / **gone up**.
10 There has been a **decline** / **drop** in sales per outlet.

Vocabulary check

1

Company Structure	Recruitment
organisation chart	applicant
headquarters	interview
IT	CV
subsidiary	head-hunter

Retailing	Franchising
department store	operation manual
discount	front end fee
mass market	royalty
range	management services fee

Management
corporate culture
authority
subordinate
decision-making

2

2 department stores
3 CVs
4 head-hunter
5 interview
6 decision-making
7 subordinates
8 range
9 headquarters
10 corporate culture

3

2 am responsible for
3 report to
4 collaborate with
5 been involved in
6 work on
7 succeeded in
8 result in
9 believe in
10 benefit from

unit 6

Banking

Key vocabulary

This section gives an overview of the banking system in the United Kingdom and explains some of the major differences between the various institutions that operate in this sector. This outline can be used as an introduction and then, if necessary, the specific roles of these institutions can be described in greater detail. Check that students understand the technical vocabulary such as *deposit, mergers, acquisitions, monetary policy* and *loan*. You may wish to ask students to close their books and fill the gaps in the photocopiable vocabulary exercise on page 68 after listening to the cassette version.

Lead-in

1 This short pair work activity gives students the chance to discuss the different services that banks in their country make available and also to see which of these they actually use. While students are working on this, go round the class offering assistance to those students who may have difficulty finding the correct English terms for some of the services they use. It may be useful to explain such terms as *overdraft, savings account, mortgages, online banking*, and the verbs *borrow* and *withdraw*, which students will need to use later in this unit.

2 This interview allows students to compare their own lists with the range of services that are offered by a local bank branch such as HSBC. The comparison between this bank's principal operations and those of banks in students' countries should reveal some significant differences concerning such things as opening hours, the availability of insurance and investments and the use of automated or electronic banking systems. Students may have difficulty with the following: *investment products, back office processing, barristers, solicitors.*

TAPESCRIPT:

Well, my name's Eleanor Stevens, I'm the manager here at the HSBC Bank in Chancery Lane in London. I've been in the bank for fifteen years and I've only been in this branch about three months.

At this branch we have approximately 6,000 customers, and our basic opening hours are Monday to Friday, 9.30 to 4.30. This branch actually isn't open on Saturdays but many of our branches are, where there's a need for it in the local community. But on Saturdays mostly the branches are open between 9.30 and 3.30, and if cash transactions are undertaken on that day, they're not processed until the following business day, obviously, usually the Monday.

The main services we offer to customers here are the usual: loans, mortgages, savings, investment products. And we also do quite a lot of foreign business for our customers where we send money abroad or we receive it from abroad.

We have thirty members of staff, which is quite large for branches these days because a lot of our back office processing is done in central sites away from the branch, which obviously costs money in terms of rent.

Erm, the role of our bank in the community is that we get involved, and in this particular community it's the legal community, very many barristers and solicitors, and most of them are our clients here.

So it's a very nice place to be, and it's a very nice set of customers, and we enjoy it.

KEY:

Location:	Chancery Lane, London
Number of customers:	approximately 6,000
Opening hours:	9.30–4.30 Monday–Friday
Services offered:	loans, mortgages, savings, investment products and foreign business
Number of employees:	30
Role in the community:	to get involved, particularly in the legal community

3 KEY:

1 j	**3** d	**5** g	**7** c	**9** b
2 h	**4** e	**6** a	**8** f	**10** i

4 KEY:

1 a bank statement
2 traveller's cheques
3 a bill
4 chequebook
5 cash machine or cashpoint

Reading

1 As the text actually deals with banking services that are offered to business customers, this pre-reading exercise is designed to develop students' awareness of the different sorts of services that companies require from their banks. Students should be able to prepare a list which might include:

business loans	high interest deposit account
payment services	references
insurance: life assurance, commercial insurance	overdrafts
pension planning	investment assistance
telephone banking	international services
online or electronic banking	leasing
current account	mortgages

2 This text is from a Bank of Scotland brochure presenting HOBS (Home and Office Banking Service) for business customers. The brochure is designed to attract the attention of potential customers and to inform them of the advantages that HOBS can offer them. The first part of the text is written in a lively, fast-paced narrative style to illustrate the stress of running a company and to show how HOBS can make it easier for company managers to get the latest information in order to manage their companies' finances as well as possible. The second part of the text simply lists the different features and benefits of the system. Students may also have difficulties with the following:

Idiomatic expression: *at your fingertips* (line 10)

The principal difficulties in the text are lexical rather than grammatical and concern words that will be referred to in the different vocabulary sections. A note has been added at the end of the text to explain what is meant by BACS and CHAPS which are standard banking services that are available in the UK.

Students should scan the text first to check how many of the things on their lists are actually mentioned before moving on to sections 3 and 4.

3 KEY:

2 e Convenience
3 b Cost-effectiveness
4 a Security
5 c Flexibility
6 f Priority Payments

4 KEY:

1 F
2 F
3 T
4 T
5 F

Vocabulary

1 KEY:

Across

1 direct debits
6 net
9 wages
10 routine
12 cost
18 fit
20 foreign currency

Down

1 distribution
2 banking
3 transactions
5 reporting
7 urgent
8 data
11 control
13 transfer
14 funds
15 price
16 open
19 pay

2 KEY:

2 deposit
3 cheque
4 debit
5 cash
6 payment
7 debit card
8 credit
9 transactions
10 balance

3 Computer-related words and expressions in the text:

boot up (line 8)
laptop (line 8)
downloaded (line 9)
central computers (lines 9–10)
search criteria (line 28)
off-line processing (line 39)
PC (line 42)
access (line 43)
software (line 48)
re-key (line 54)
database (line 55)
computerised payments (footnote)

KEY:

2 laptop
3 download
4 search criteria
5 processing
6 software
7 re-key

Vocabulary development: abbreviations

1 Abbreviations are used in all areas of business and this exercise simply presents some of the most common ones that are used in correspondence and in business documents.

time	money	people
p.a. (per annum) GMT (Greenwich Mean Time) a.m. (ante meridiem)*	VAT (Value Added Tax) IOU (I Owe You) SFr (Swiss Franc) PAYE (Pay as You Earn)	MD (Managing Director) CEO (Chief Executive Officer)

companies	other
Ltd (Limited) Corp (Corporation) plc (public limited company)	i.e. (id est)* e.g. (exempli gratia)* AGM (Annual General Meeting) N/A (Not Applicable or Not Available) AOB (Any Other Business) asap (As Soon As Possible)

* The full forms of these abbreviations are very rarely used.

2 KEY: (suggested answers only)

time p.m. (post meridiem)
money USD (US dollars)
people CFO (Chief Finance Officer)
companies Inc. (Incorporated)
other RSVP, VIP

Language Focus

Allow, enable, let

This is a simple grammar point but one which often leads to confusion due to the fact that the verb *let* is used without *to*.

Practice

KEY: (suggested answers only)

1 A fax machine allows you to transmit and receive copies of documents rapidly.
2 A laptop computer lets you work while you are travelling.
3 A mobile phone allows you to make and receive calls wherever you are.
4 A modem enables computers to exchange data.
5 A credit card lets you buy goods on credit.
6 E-mail enables you to send and receive messages and files via your computer.

First and second conditional

This section provides a short review of the differences between the two forms. For further information students should consult page 166 of the Grammar Reference material in the Student's Book.

KEY:

1 Sentence **A** is an example of the **first conditional**. The conditional clause *(if...)* refers to a situation that **may possibly happen**.
2 Sentence **B** is an example of the **second conditional**. The conditional clause *(if...)* refers to a situation that **is unlikely to happen** or **is unreal**.

Practice

1 The answers that students give in this exercise will depend on which of these situations they are more or less likely to encounter. It is possible to use both conditional forms in all of the sentences except sentence 4 where the second conditional form sounds more natural.

KEY:

2 If I lose my credit card, I will inform the bank immediately.
2 If I lost my credit card, I would inform the bank immediately.
3 If I need some money, I will ask the bank manager for a loan.
3 If I needed some money, I would ask the bank manager for a loan.
4 If I found any mistakes on my bank statement, I would change to a different bank.
5 If I earn more money, I will be able to save more.
5 If I earned more money, I would be able to save more.
6 If I order a chequebook, will I get it before the end of the week?
6 If I ordered a chequebook, would I get it before the end of the week?

2 The problems that are presented here are unreal situations which we can talk about using the second conditional form only. Encourage pairs of students to explain what they would do in such situations and get them to ask questions and give reactions to what their partners have to say. There are many alternatives in each case which could include:

I'd speak to him about it.

I'd try to contact the railway company first.

I'd ask Head Office for instructions.

I'd refuse the position.

I'd ask my lawyer to contact them.

I'd contact my bank and my employer and ask them what to do.

Business Skills Focus: Negotiating

Reading

1 This short questionnaire draws attention to some of the key attitudes and behaviours that are important for negotiating to be successful. Students' answers here will enable them to identify what they need to improve in order to become a better negotiator.

2 The ten questions deal with the following skills, attitudes and behaviours:

1 Self-control is a key quality – you should be careful not to let emotional reactions influence your judgement.

2 Being able to reach a compromise is a critical ingredient and it is important to understand that you may have to make concessions.

3 Understanding the position of the other side is essential if you are going to reach an agreement.

4 Allowing time for arguments to be developed and not making hasty decisions are two important qualities.

5 Distinguishing what is important from what is not helps to focus on the main issues.

6 Reacting calmly to criticism will help to increase the chances of a successful outcome.

7 Doing the background research before entering a negotiation means that you will be able to anticipate problems that may arise and the positions people will adopt on certain issues.

8 Looking for a solution that can benefit both parties is the key to win-win negotiating.

9 Being able to deal with stress will enable you to remain composed during a negotiation.

10 Listening carefully to what people have to say is essential in order to understand exactly what they are expecting from you and to seek clarification where necessary.

For further information on 'Negotiating', see the Business Skills photocopiable section on page 76.

Listening

1 This first exercise is designed to get students to listen to the dialogue as a whole in order to set the context and register.

TAPESCRIPT:

Bank manager:
Mr Cowan, I'd just like to say that I am very pleased with the latest figures that you provided. Your business has really got off to a good start. I mean you've almost doubled the number of visitors to your site during the last two months which is very encouraging. And I see that you now have several thousand regular customers in the United Kingdom. Is that right?

Mark Cowan:
Yes. In fact we are at more than three thousand. I think it shows that we've finally got the format right and that we are offering a service that suits our target audience. So we have decided to start working on the next phase i.e. expanding and improving both the site itself and the services that we provide, in a number of ways. We're planning to include more practical advice for customers. We're also thinking of hiring someone to look after the maintenance and technical development side. So that's why I'd like to know if you would be prepared to extend our bank loan to cover these costs.

Bank manager:
Well, I'm afraid that I can't give you an answer on that right now. I mean I think that there are some things that we'd need to look at in detail before I'd be able to decide that.

Mark Cowan:
What exactly are you referring to?

Bank manager:
I'd like to see the figures for the last two months and I'd be particularly interested in having a look at the statistics for late payment and credit card fraud. You'd also need to show me some new projections based on actual performance so I could compare them with the original ones.

Mark Cowan:
OK. I think I should be able to put all that together by the end of the week. When would you like to arrange to meet?

Bank manager:
Well, let's say in two weeks from now. Is that OK with you?

Mark Cowan:
That's fine. I'll confirm by phone.

KEY:

a He is meeting the bank manager to discuss the possibility of extending the company's bank loan.
b He avoids making a firm commitment until he has the relevant information.

2 It is important that students listen carefully to the functional language that the speakers use to explain their positions. Draw attention to the way that conditional structures and modal verbs are included at different points in the negotiation. Remind students that they will need to assimilate this language and use it in the negotiations that they will be conducting themselves in the speaking section of this activity.

KEY:

2 B 'Well, I'm afraid …'
3 M 'What exactly are you referring to?'
4 B 'You'd also need to show me …'
5 M 'OK.'
6 B 'Is that OK with you?'

Role-play

This activity allows students to apply what they have learned about negotiating and the appropriate language for negotiating in English. The preparation phase is particularly important and both sides should have a clear idea of what their objectives are for the negotiation and what information they need to obtain before making a decision. This will involve preparing appropriate questions and anticipating potential problems.

There is an additional photocopiable role-play on pages 76–78. This material includes useful notes on listening and speaking together with a list of expressions to use during negotiations.

Writing

The report should simply state the context of the negotiation and then list the conclusions that were reached and the conditions that were imposed. Remind students that, as they will need to use reported speech to summarise what was said, they should consult the Grammar Reference section on page 169 of the Student's Book for assistance with reported speech forms.

unit 7

Business and the Environment

Key vocabulary

This section gives an overview of environmental issues that can affect businesses. Check that students understand the vocabulary in bold. You may wish to ask them to close their books and fill the gaps in the photocopiable vocabulary exercise on page 69 after listening to the cassette version.

Lead-in

1 This Lead-in section presents students with a selection of cartoons which depict some of the environmental problems we are facing in the world today. They were published in the World Press Review and were part of an exhibition entitled 'Our Endangered Planet' held in Moscow. Before discussing the cartoons, introduce students to the basic vocabulary of the environment such as *ozone layer, global warming, oil spills* and *nuclear waste*. Check that students understand the questions and encourage them to give reasons for their answers. This could lead into a class discussion.

2 Students are now asked to discuss the role that business can play in environmental concerns, based on the three statements provided. Before reading the statements, ask students if they have ever read or heard about companies being sued or rewarded for their policies concerning the environment. They may have heard about oil tanker disasters, or they may have seen advertising campaigns based on a company's contribution to the environment, such as washing powder without phosphates or companies who recycle their products, etc. Ask if they have heard of Anita Roddick – she is the founder of a successful retail chain of body and skin care products, The Body Shop. It is the ultimate 'green' company involved in campaigning on major environmental concerns. Encourage students to give their opinion of the statements. Finish with a class discussion.

3 This provides concrete examples of companies' policies and introduces more vocabulary. Students can do this in pairs first.

KEY:

1 a cosmetics firm
2 a fast food chain
3 a sports footwear firm
4 a car manufacturer

Students could think of local companies with environmental policies.

Reading

1 Start by asking students what they know, if anything, about Patagonia. You may need to explain some of the more complicated vocabulary, such as *corporate culture, radical environmentalism* and *sound business practices*.

Website: www.patagonia.com

Suggested questions:

How does Patagonia express its ethic of 'radical' environmentalism? or
What sorts of 'radical' activities are Patagonia involved in?

Has Patagonia succeeded in making a 10% pre-tax profit while caring about the environment?

How are their products environmentally-friendly?

What exactly do the Patagonia people mean by 'sound business practices'?

What do they mean by 'social good'? or How do they measure the 'social good' they do?

Do they recycle their products?

2 Encourage students to read the text only for the answers to their questions.

3 Students should now read in more detail. Ask students to say where they found their answers. They may have difficulties with the following:

Vocabulary: *fleece* (para 1) *activism* (para 11) *sporting* (para 12)

Idiomatic expressions: *takes pains to explain* (para 3) *the big picture* (para 3) *green* (para 6)

KEY:

1 Patagonia's customers are loyal because the company has a very powerful communication policy.
2 Patagonia publishes high quality advertising and company literature which contain detailed essays about the environmental policies of the company.
3 Patagonia's objective is to convince consumers that it is better to buy environmentally-friendly products, even if they are more expensive.
4 Patagonia publishes the results of its internal environmental assessment. In it, customers can read about the company's efforts to respect both the environment and the working conditions of their employees.
5 Consumers respond very positively to the grants programme and write in to the company to inform them of their personal environmental success stories.

Vocabulary

1 Encourage students to find the words in the passage and guess the meanings before doing the exercise. Check understanding and pronunciation.

KEY:

2 c catalogs
3 b product descriptions
4 f organic
5 d empower
6 a sustainability

2 Some students may need more guidance here. Encourage them to look at context, perhaps give clues such as the first letter.

KEY:

2 knowledgeable
3 conventional
4 strategic
5 linked
6 contributed
7 nationwide
8 successes

3 This exercise focuses on common 'business' collocations in the text. You should check understanding with questions.

KEY:

2 e doubt claims
3 c publish results
4 a conduct business
5 b raise awareness

4 This provides practice of the collocations in 3. You could ask students to write more sentences using the new vocabulary.

KEY:

2 conducts its business
3 publish the results
4 raise … awareness
5 doubt claims

Vocabulary development: word building

1 Before looking at the exercise write 'environment' on the board and elicit possible changes to the word to show the number of possibilities. Look at the examples from the text and focus on changes in form and pronunciation. If time is short, allocate words to pairs or groups. Go round and help where necessary.

KEY:

a production
b producer
c productive
d progress
e progressive
f management
g manager
h managerial
i direction
j director
k direct

2 Again, this could be allocated to groups or set for homework. Encourage students to come up with realistic, feasible words.

KEY:

a developed / developer / developing / development / developmental
b committed / commitment
c sustained / sustainable / sustainability
d employed / employment / employer / employee / employable

Discussion

Encourage students to justify their answers. Students could follow this up with a short written reply for homework to consolidate the language learnt.

Language Focus

Expressing contrast

1 You may wish to do this before the discussion so that students could use the language in the discussion. Introduce this with a simple statement on the board, such as:

Buying green is expensive – Good for the environment.

Elicit possible words then go to examples in the book. You may want to refer students to the Grammar Reference material on page 167 of the Student's Book.

KEY:

2 c
3 b
4 a
5 d

2 Use students' answers to **a** and **b** to highlight the patterns.

KEY:

a *Although* and *even though* are followed by a subject + verb.
b *Despite* and *In spite of* are followed by a noun or verb + *-ing*.

Practice

KEY: (suggested answers only)

1 Even though young people are concerned about the environment, they can't always afford environmentally-friendly products.
2 In spite of Patagonia's efforts to convince other companies to use organically-grown cotton, many companies resist because it costs more.
3 Despite rising pollution in Paris, people still prefer to take their cars to work.
4 Despite the fact that many countries organise separate waste collections for glass, paper, metal and plastic, many others don't.
5 Although most beauty products carry the label 'against animal testing' some of the components may have been tested on animals.

The passive

Again, you could use a simple example on the board to introduce the language before going to the examples in the book. Encourage students to look at the material in the Grammar Reference Section on page 167 of the Student's Book.

KEY:

A The verb is in the active form. The emphasis is on *how* oil is saved.
B The verb is in the passive form. The emphasis is on *the fact* that they are recycled, not on *how*.

Practice

1 Check students understand the vocabulary in the leaflet. Ask students to look at the pictures and text to describe the process in active form, then go on to the passives.

KEY:

2 is converted
3 chopped
4 are melted
5 are shipped
6 are made

2 KEY:

1 More and more 'environmentally-friendly' products will be bought.
2 Plastic bottles should be taken to the local recycling centre.
3 150 synchilla garments can be made from 3,700 bottles.
4 A new item has recently been added to the product range.
5 Green-marketing strategies are being developed by many companies.

Skills Focus

Listening

Ask students to imagine what reasons people may have for going to the Body Shop. Pause after each extract and play it again if necessary. Point out that the speakers were interviewed outside a Body Shop in London, and therefore use a very conversational style and sometimes speak quickly. Ask students what they think of the reasons given by the speakers and if their own buying decisions are based on the same kinds of considerations.

TAPESCRIPT:

Speaker 1:
Because I believe that nothing should be tested on animals and I believe what they do must be having some good effect on the environment, so that's why I buy them.

Speaker 2:
Because as I've said, I've been using it for ten years (most of their products for ten years), and they suit my skin and skin type.

Speakers 3 and 4:
I think that's the major part of it, not testing and the lack of packaging. It makes the choice easier rather than having to read gallons and gallons of packaging. You have a guarantee that it's not tested on animals as well, because other places, they tell you but you're not quite sure.

Speaker 5:
Well I like the shops, I think they're very nice, so it's a nice place to be. So probably, that really, the presentation, the packaging, the sort of ideas behind the whole thing.

Speaker 6:
The stuff's good, and also the packaging's very nice for presents.

Speaker 7:
Economic reasons, generally they're a fairly reasonable price. Like the packaging – simple, less waste.

Speaker 8:
I suppose, you know, the name is quite well established and so you go for something that obviously somebody else has tried before you, you know.

KEY: (suggested information for answers)

Customers' reasons for buying Body Shop products:

1 This customer buys Body Shop products because she is against testing on animals and also because she feels that the Body Shop is having a good effect on the environment.
2 Body Shop products suit this customer's skin.
3 and 4 These customers appreciate the lack of packaging and the fact that products are not tested on animals.
5 This customer finds the shops themselves pleasant to shop in, and also likes the way products are presented and packaged.
6 This customer likes the quality of the products and thinks they make good presents.
7 The price and the packaging correspond to this customer's demands.
8 This customer buys the products for their established brand name and good reputation.

Speaking

1 The remainder of the Skills Focus is based on the role of companies sponsoring worthy causes. Check that students understand the introduction, then give or elicit one or two examples to get students started. Round off with ideas on each point.

2 This activity offers students an opportunity to consider the advantages that sponsoring offers a company. Students should read each project and decide in groups which one most appeals to them. Ensure that groups have not chosen the same project. All the projects could appeal to a computer company looking for an event to sponsor and it is for students to justify that appeal.

3 Go through the introduction and checklist, dealing with vocabulary.

The groups should then consider each of the ten questions provided in the checklist that a company would use when deciding which project to sponsor. Go around the different groups checking that this is being done in a systematic way. Encourage them to take notes on each point they discuss as they will need these to complete the writing task which follows.

Writing

1 Go through the model, making the organisation clear to students to help them complete this task. Check that students keep to the layout and that they present their arguments in a clear and persuasive manner. There is a photocopiable model of a letter asking for sponsorship on page 79.

2 Students take on the role of the directors of a company looking for an environmental cause to sponsor. Make sure that each group reads and makes notes on all the request letters. You may need to photocopy them to ensure this. They could select a spokesperson to say which one they like best and why. The other groups may wish to contest the decisions and should be encouraged to give their opinions. Note down any mistakes and, following the discussion, provide feedback on errors made.

unit 8

The Stock Market

Key vocabulary

This section provides a basic introduction to the stock market. The topic itself is complex and this unit contains some quite difficult vocabulary, some of which is specific to either the United Kingdom or the United States. You may wish to start by asking students if they can explain what the stock exchange/market is and how it works. Once this has been done, the class can read through the Key vocabulary section. Alternatively, you may wish to ask students to close their books and fill the gaps in the photocopiable exercise on page 69 after listening to the cassette version.

The stock market is currently changing very rapidly in a number of ways. It is now possible to buy and sell shares using computer terminals and many countries now have electronic market places. In addition to this, investors can now trade directly over the Internet. Lastly, the stock market has become increasingly international in scope, which has meant not only extended opening hours, but has also led to a number of alliances between international exchanges.

Lead-in

1 This section introduces students to the language commonly found in the financial pages of the press.

If possible, bring in an English language newspaper and read some of the financial headlines to the class. Draw attention to the less standard forms of *increase* and *decrease* that are used to describe share performance on the stock market such as *slide*, *slip* and *plummet*.

KEY:

Good performance: **1**, **3**, **4** and **7**

Poor performance: **2**, **5**, **6** and **8**

2 In this short listening extract, students are invited to listen to a personal investor's experience of investing on the stock market and note down the type of investments and the reasons for investing. They may need to listen a few times as they are introduced to some new vocabulary here. It is important to point out that Americans generally refer to *shares* as *stock*. When students have completed the table, you could ask them to explain why Isobel Mendelson decided against buying bonds.

TAPESCRIPT: (part 1)

When I decided to invest on the stock exchange, I got advice from a broker on the type of investments to make. She told me that it was really important to diversify so I did, both geographically and sector wise. I invested in Europe and the United States and have stock in almost every business sector. I have preferred stock and stocks in Healthcare, Food, Transportation, Banking and the Information Technology sector.

I decided against buying bonds. Government Bonds are only interesting when you live in the States because you pay less tax there if you buy bonds from the government. However, as I live in Europe, I prefer to buy 'preferred stock'. They have to be bought through a broker and are similar to bonds as it is like making a loan to a company instead of to the government. The company pays you back before paying common stock or ordinary shares. However, they are riskier than bonds but the returns are much higher – 7 to 8.5. I prefer to take the risk and get higher returns.

KEY:

Types of investment	Reasons for investing
Preferred stock and stocks in various business and geographical sectors	High returns on high risk investments

The next listening extract provides information about the 'Internet portfolio trackers'. You may wish to explain that when we refer to all of an individual's or company's investments on the stock exchange, we use the phrase *financial portfolio*.

TAPESCRIPT: (part 2)

My broker looks after my investments but I like to keep up-to-date with them. In fact, I check on them several times a day! I track them on the Internet. There are lots of 'Internet portfolio trackers' now. I use the CBS one. You have to enter in the number of stocks you have, the symbol of each company, the price you paid and the date you bought them. Then it will give you your profits and losses. In fact the information on how your stocks are doing is updated every five minutes!

KEY:

She checks on her shares regularly on the Internet through the CBS portfolio tracker.

Reading

1 Students may need some encouraging questions to get them discussing what they think the text is about, such as *What do you think is meant by the term 'investment fever'? How are investing and the Internet linked? What kinds of things can you buy on the Internet? Do you think it is possible to buy stocks and shares on the Internet? etc.*

2 Students are asked to read the text to see if they have guessed correctly what the main ideas of the text are. They may have difficulties with the following:

Vocabulary: *going* (line 58)

Idiomatic expression: *setting their sights on* (lines 25–6)

3 KEY:

1 People are taking more interest in the stock exchange because they realise that they must take responsibility for their own financial futures. Therefore they must think carefully about their savings and find a way to gain the maximum return on their money.
2 American brokers are interested in Europe as an alternative market to exploit. They are making less and less money in America due to heavy competition which is driving down their profit margins.
3 The American brokers operating in Europe are cautious not to offend European regulators.
4 European traders are preparing to fight off American competition. They are launching 'online' services of their own.
5 In the long-term, the Americans will find themselves in the same position in Europe as they are in America today. The high competition, partly created by them, on the European market will drive down European profit margins, just as it did in America.

Vocabulary

1 KEY:

2 i	4 g	6 a	8 f	10 b
3 h	5 j	7 d	9 c	

2 KEY:

2 broker	4 dividends	6 shareholder
3 shares	5 commission	

Vocabulary development: phrasal verbs 1

1 Here students are asked to distinguish between transitive and intransitive phrasal verbs.

KEY:

a transitive

2 KEY:

b buy up	f pointed out
c looking after	g call on
d go about	h let down
e think over	

Language Focus

The third conditional

Encourage students to look at the Grammar Reference material on page 167 of the Student's Book.

KEY:

A	1 the past	2 No	3 No
B	1 the past	2 Yes	3 Yes

Practice

KEY:

1 If I had been an assistant manager, I would have earned £5 an hour.
2 If I had taken flight BD493 to Paris, I would have arrived on time.
3 If I had sold my Renault in 1997, I would have got £10,000 for it.
4 If I had waited until 1999 to buy my PC, I would have paid £975.
5 If I hadn't sold my M & S shares, I would have received dividends of 6.5p in 1999.

Yet, still, already

KEY:

a still   b already   c yet   d yet

Practice

KEY:

2 I am **still** thinking about investing money on the stock market but can't make up my mind.
3 I have contacted a broker **already** and he has given some very good advice.
4 He **still** hasn't bought anything on the European exchanges.
5 I'm very pleased with my shares; they've gone up **already**.
6 Now that you've lost so much money, do you **still** think it's a good idea to invest on the stock exchange?

Skills Focus

Reading

This section presents the complex information contained in the share price listings found in most newspapers. It would be useful to read each explanation through with students, focusing particularly on the listing for Unilever shares which is highlighted by way of example.

Once students have understood the explanation they may begin working in pairs on the share listings taken from *The Independent*. Go around to each group and provide help where necessary.

KEY:

1

b 714.0   c 107.5   d 185.5

2

Food producers: Associated British foods (-38)
Gas distribution: British Gas (-5.5)
Health care: Seton Scholl (+24)
Household goods: Reckitt & C (+24)

Insurance: Allied Zurich (+29)

3

c Reckitt & C (300 pence down on its highest price for the year)

4

a Euclidian (14.9) b Cox insurance (1.4)

5

a 12.5 b 26.8 c 15.9 d 18.5

Listening

1 This short pre-listening exercise focuses on the prepositions used after expressions of increase and decrease. Illustrate this point by writing an example on the board: *The average price of a Paris-London flight* ***increased/rose by*** *£50.*

The same information can be expressed by using a noun form + of: *There was* ***a(n) increase/rise of*** *£50 in the average price of a Paris-London flight.*

We specify the highest and lowest figures as follows: *The average price* ***increased/rose from*** *£150* ***to*** *£200.*

Students should study the table carefully before deciding which prepositions to use.

KEY:

2 to	4 at	6 up
3 down	5 by	7 of

Note: In the second sentence, only the final result of the increase/decrease is given. This is a common feature of stock market reports.

The prepositions *up* and *down* are commonly used when describing increase and decrease in share prices. When there has been no change in share prices, we can use the expression *to stand at.*

2 Students should now be ready to listen to the taped passage, which should be played as many times as required to extract the relevant information. Students should be given about five minutes to make the calculations required for the Change column after which the correct answers can be given.

TAPESCRIPT:

Avis Europe shares rose from 246p yesterday to 253p. British Energy shares decreased from 688p to 654p. Rolls Royce shares were up 2p at 247p and Cookson's shares also increased 7p to 132.5p, while Tesco's shares were up 1p at 179p. There was a decrease of 2p in British Aerospace shares which are now at 512p. BSkyB shares fell 9.5p to 510p while Alsthom stood at 140p.

KEY:

Name of the share	Yesterday's closing price	Today's closing price	Change
British Energy	688p	654p	-34
Rolls Royce	245p	247p	+2
Cookson	125.5p	132.5p	+7
Tesco	178p	179p	+1
British Aerospace	514p	512p	-2
BSkyB	519.5p	510p	-9.5
Alsthom	140p	140p	–

Speaking

1 and **2** This activity provides further practice in reading share listings and enables students to express hypothetical situations in the past using the third conditional. Students should realise that they are not being asked to choose shares as specialists. However, depending on recent trends they will probably be aware of the fact that certain sectors or companies are in difficulty and therefore should avoid choosing them. It should take students about ten minutes to choose their shares and then an additional five minutes to check the more recent listings on page 158 of the Student's Book and work out the profit and loss they would have made. Students who would have made a particularly sound (or unwise) investment should be asked to present their findings to the rest of the class. Make sure the third conditional is used correctly.

Writing

1, 2 and 3 are preparation steps for stage 4. The first step is to get students thinking about what affects share prices. When they read the extract in 2, they will see that profits are falling and jobs are being cut in the company and that this has a negative affect on share prices.

3 This provides students with a sample summary. To make this step more active, students are asked to correct the mistakes.

KEY:

Profits are down not up.

They are decreasing, not increasing, the number of employees.

Share prices fell in value, they did not rise.

4 For the final stage ask students to bring in a daily newspaper. Ensure you have a selection of newspapers yourself so that every student has access to one. You may prefer to use the photocopiable articles and models of summaries on page 80.

unit 9

Import Export

Key vocabulary

As an introduction to the topic of this unit, ask students if they can name any international trade bodies such as WTO or EFTA. You may also choose to start up a discussion based on any recent trends, such as negotiations, agreements or conflicts involving 'trade wars/sanctions' between two or more countries. The class should then read through the Key vocabulary section. Alternatively, you may wish to ask students to close their books and fill the gaps in the photocopiable exercise on page 70 after listening to the cassette version.

Lead-in

1 Students should start by discussing why countries trade. What are their country's main imports/exports? The listening provides a more in-depth look at the fundamental principle of international trading. Allow time for students to read the questions first. You may need to play this more than once.

TAPESCRIPT:

They trade because it's in their interest to trade. It's the same reason that individuals trade. Individuals are trading all the time. Now, let me give you a kind of, an example for that, of that. You would not think it was sensible if you spent all your time growing your own food because you would have to work 20 hours a day. You don't have the expertise maybe to do that, and you don't have the land to do that or at least it's not good land and therefore it makes more sense to you to do what it is that you do best, OK, and in the process earning enough to buy whatever food you then need. And therefore if individuals are doing what er, what they do best, they are in a position to make best use of their resources, of their own abilities, of their own talents and therefore earn more and that allows them to buy what it is they don't produce themselves, and the same logic, exactly the same logic applies to countries.

KEY:

1 He compares countries to individuals.
2 He uses the example of growing one's own food.
3 Countries should specialise in what they do most efficiently (i.e. where they can best use their resources) and buy what they don't produce themselves.

2 The chart gives a history of the EU, a significant trading block. Before looking at it, write EEC/EC/EU on the board. Ask students to say what they stand for, they can then read and check. Ask students if any more countries have joined since the table was written.

3 The Europe quiz is designed to get students to think about the different geographical, economic and cultural characteristics of the EU countries.

Find out what made students come to their decisions and whether they are surprised by some of the 'real' answers.

KEY:

1 France (549,000 square km)
2 Germany (81.14 million inhabitants)
3 Ireland (15.1% p.a.)
4 Netherlands (forecasts are 399 inhabitants per square km for 2020)
5 Germany (approximately 17.5% of France's total exports goes to Germany)
6 Germany (approximately 10.2% of Sweden's exports goes to Germany)
7 a) United Kingdom
b) France
c) Germany
d) Spain
8 a) Most: France (more than 1,5 million tonnes) Least: Luxembourg
b) Most: United Kingdom (approx. 40 kg per head p.a.) Least: Spain
c) Most: Italy (approx. 58.5 litres per head p.a.) Least: Ireland
d) Most: Greece (7.70 smoked per head per day) Least: Netherlands
9 France
10 Finland (76% of land is covered in forest)
11 Germany (approx. 7,000 magazines) *Stern*, *Der Spiegel*
12 Finland
13 Netherlands (36½ days per year, compared to 22 in Portugal and Greece)
14 Netherlands: Royal Dutch Petroleum

Reading

1 The text gives a profile of the Belgian electronics company BARCO. Since 1994, BARCO has been best known for its digital projectors for computers. They started to export to India ten years ago and exports now account for a significant part of their BFr 23bn turnover. In the text we learn about how they developed their export strategy.

You may want to ask students to guess what methods a company could use to get into India, before they read and find out.

Students may have difficulties with the following:
Vocabulary: *strategic focus* (para 2) *niche markets* (para 3)

KEY:

In the text we find examples of nearly all the methods mentioned except for a joint-venture project:

BARCO started by working with local agents to sell kits for video monitors (para 4). After that it set up its own sales office (para 4) and then set up an assembly plant (para 5).

2 Students read in more detail to complete this task.

KEY:

Advantages	Disadvantages
Exciting long-term market opportunities	*Complex market*
People speak English	*More closed than other fast growing economies*
Fascinating country	*Tax barriers and delays*
One fifth of the world's population lives there	*A lot of bureaucracy and paperwork*
	Deceptive cultural hurdles

Vocabulary

1 Check students' understanding and pronunciation.

KEY:

2 assembled
3 a shift
4 niche market
5 exploit
6 obstacles
7 bureaucracy
8 delays

2 This practises vocabulary from the unit so far, and gives another example of a company trying to break into the Indian market.

KEY:

2 assemble
3 niche market
4 delays
5 tariffs
6 obstacles
7 licences

Vocabulary development: compound adjectives 1

Ask students to see how quickly they can find a compound adjective in the previous text.

1 Students may want to do the first part, forming the adjectives, before going on to match them to the nouns.

KEY:

b old-fashioned typewriter
c short-term opportunities
d low-budget advertising
e well-known personality
f high-level decision-making
g user-friendly software
h well-trained staff

2 There are hundreds of this type of adjective: *right-wing, high-powered, high-ranking, high-pressure, high-profile, open-minded, open-plan, over-optimistic, full-time, fully-fledged (full-fledged* – US), *all-inclusive, all-powerful, all-round*, etc.

Listening

The purpose of this exercise is to introduce students to the invoice and the bill of lading, important documents commonly used in the context of importing and exporting. Ask students if they know what an invoice is. Have they ever received one? Have they used them at work?

The invoice

Allow time for students to ask questions about vocabulary, such as *issue, freight* or *warehouse*. Play the tape more than once if necessary. This gives students an opportunity to revise numbers, a point dealt with in Unit 1, and the alphabet.

TAPESCRIPT:

By looking at the invoice number 699, you will notice that on the 7th May 1999, the Metropolitan Tennis Equipment Company of Los Angeles shipped a total of 160 tennis rackets to Champion Sport Ltd. in London. The shipment included 120 of the GX12 model priced at £78 and 40 of the 'Tennis Pro' model at £116, for a total of £14,000. The cost of freight was £500 and the insurance from warehouse to warehouse was £90. Hence, the total amount to be paid by the UK importer was £14,590. The rackets were packed in 16 cardboard cartons, 10 per carton, on which the words MET CS LTD. LONDON 1–16 were written. The import licence number was BRX 43 1999. The invoice was signed by an official of the exporting company, Mr Robert Morales.

KEY:

2 699
3 160
4 120
5 40
6 £14,000
7 £500
8 £90
9 £14,590
10 16
11 10
12 BRX 43 1999

Reading

The bill of lading

Students should first study the document carefully and check they understand the parts of the document they are being asked to identify. Ask students if they can see what a bill of lading is used for.

KEY:

2 b 3 f 4 c 5 h 6 e 7 a 8 d

Language Focus

The future

Encourage students to look at the Grammar Reference material on pages 167–8 of the Student's Book.

KEY:

1 f 2 c 3 e 4 a 5 b 6 d

Practice

KEY:

1 'll get
2 am going to leave
3 'll have
4 are going to need
5 are going to visit
6 will be

Describing trends

This is a revision point from Unit 1 and also deals with adjectives and adverbs. Elicit nouns and verbs and then ask if students know which adjectives and adverbs can be used.

KEY:

b gradually
c steadily (draw attention to the change from *y* to *i*)
d sharply
e dramatically (draw attention to the spelling change)
f suddenly

Practice

1 Before beginning this exercise, ask students to identify the different types of graph shown i.e. *bar chart* and *line graph*.

KEY:

2 sharply / suddenly / dramatically
3 slightly
4 gradual
5 sudden / sharp / dramatic
6 slight

2 Draw curves on the board, and ask students to match expressions to the curves. Students study the graph so that they can identify the new expressions being introduced and match them with the curves drawn on the board. If necessary, explain the meanings in words:

to fluctuate to rise and fall irregularly

to reach a peak to reach the highest point

to level off to reach stability after a period of movement

to stand at to be at a certain point at a given time

to remain stable to show no change

KEY:

b to level off: in April and September
c to remain stable: throughout September and October
d to reach a peak: at the end of January
e to stand at: at the end of the year

3 KEY:

2 e Sales fluctuated from May to September.
3 b Sales remained stable from September to November.
4 a Sales stood at 10,000 in December.
5 d Sales levelled off at about 8,000 in April.

Skills Focus

Writing

Before doing the graph interpretation exercises which follow on from here, it may be useful to review quickly the prepositions used after expressions of increase and decrease, either by having students refer to Unit 8 The Stock Market or by dictating or writing the following examples on the board, leaving out the prepositions in order to create a short gap-filling exercise.

*There was **a rise/an increase of** 3% in the unemployment rate between 1998 and 2000.*

*The number of shares traded on the stock market **rose/increased by** 15 million between November and December 2001.*

(*From … to* is used to specify the initial and final positions in a set of statistics:)

*The number of people employed in the UK shipbuilding industry **decreased/fell from** 25,000 **to** 8,000 between 1982 and 1987.*

Draw attention to the use of the past simple because in each case past trends are being described.

Students should then write a short interpretation of the graph either individually or in pairs. Make sure that the vocabulary from the previous activities is being used to describe the different trends (*to decrease steadily, to reach a peak, to level off*, etc.).

Listening

1 Let students first read the text and guess what words are missing in each gap. Are they nouns or verbs? You may need to play the tape more than once so that students can fill in the blanks in the description of the graph.

KEY/TAPESCRIPT:

In 1987 the export figures *stood at* 400 million Finnish markkaa. There was a *sharp increase* between 1987 and 1989 when figures *reached* over 800 million. This was followed by a *sharp decrease* between 1989 and 1990 when Finnish paper exports to Japan *dropped* to 400 million. There was a *slight rise* between 1990 and 1991 when exports hit the 450 million mark but they *fell* again to 400 million in 1992. Between 1992 and 1995 there was a *dramatic rise* and exports of paper to Japan *reached a peak* of 1,300 million in 1995, before *falling* again to under 1,000 million in 1997.

2 Sections of each graph are missing. Students listen to the cassette to complete them. As they listen they should plot the data on the graphs. You may need to play each description more than once, pausing after each one.

TAPESCRIPT:

Graph 1 – Wood
We can see on this graph that wood exports remained stable between 1990 and 1992 at around 50 million Finnish markkaa. Between 1992 and 1994 there was a sharp increase to 500 million where exports levelled off until 1996, then they increased dramatically again and reached a peak of 850 million by 1997.

Graph 2 – Machinery
On this second graph we see that machinery exports declined gradually between 1990 and 1992. Between 1992 and 1995, however, exports of machinery rose continually. In 1993 they were at 400 million and in 1994 they had risen to 550 million. They reached a peak of 700 million in 1995. After that, figures fell slightly to around 650 million in 1996 and levelled off at that number until 1997.

Graph 3 – Chemicals
On this third graph we notice that exports of chemicals remained stable from 1990 to 1992 at 100 million Finnish markkaa. From 1992 to 1993 there was a slight increase to 150 million. After that, exports of chemicals continued to rise steadily from 1993 to 1997. In 1995 they had reached 210 million, and in 1996, they reached a peak of 250 million and stood at this level in 1997.

KEY:

Finland's wood exports to Japan

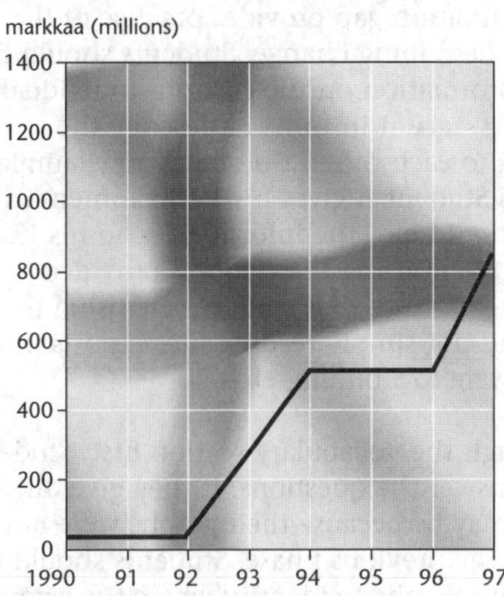

Finland's machinery exports to Japan

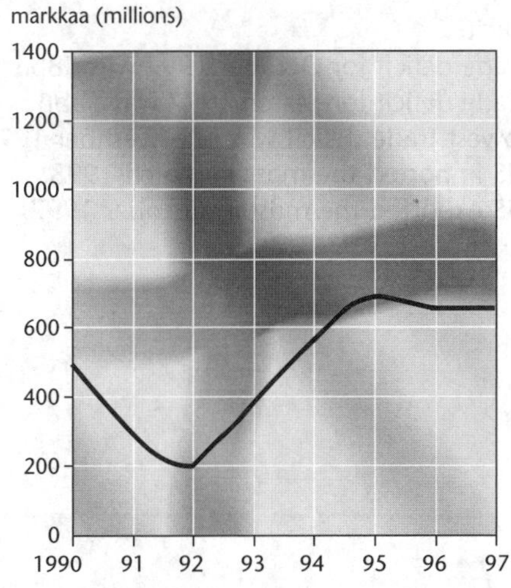

Finland's chemical exports to Japan

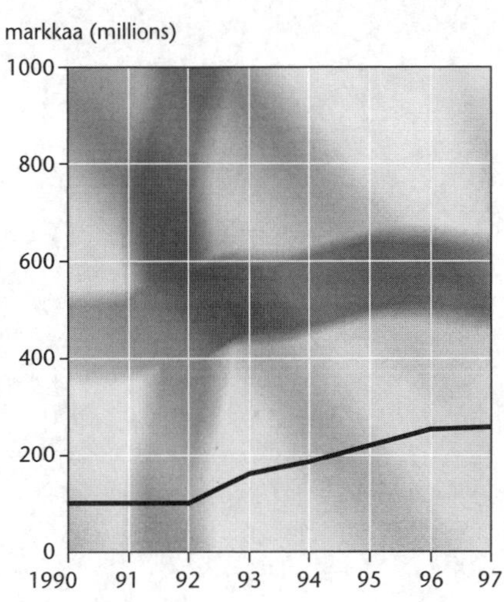

Speaking

1 This information gap provides practice of the language of describing change. Students should first study the information on their graphs individually and then, in pairs, take it in turns to describe the information to each other. Do one as an example with the class. As Student A gives his/her commentary, Student B should plot the information on his/her incomplete graph using the symbols provided. Monitor, making sure that students are using the new language and not simply reading (i.e. exports in November were $75 billion, etc.).

2 Go through the vocabulary section first. Students may then answer the questions. If they give different answers, it may be because their graphs were not drawn correctly in the previous phase. Students should then compare their graphs to identify where the error was made.

KEY:

1 Trade deficit
2 **b** The trade deficit for October 1997 was $8bn.
c The trade deficit for March 1997 was $8bn.
3 **a** The lowest trade deficit was in November 1996.
b The US imported the most in March 1998.
c The US exported the most in October 1997.

unit 10

Company Performance

Key vocabulary

This section introduces some of the basic terminology relating to the performance of a company. Although students will already be familiar with some of these terms such as *profit*, *loss* and *costs*, having studied them in previous units, the distinction between *management accounts* and *financial accounts* will be new to them. Stress that the presentation of company accounts and accountancy procedures vary considerably from country to country. This unit concentrates mainly on the information that American-listed companies are required to provide by law – it also includes the British equivalents of these. Add that the whole question of harmonising the reporting procedures for companies is an important issue for the future of international business. You may wish to ask students to close their books and fill the gaps in the photocopiable exercise on page 70 after listening to the cassette version.

Lead-in

1 Ask students what they know about PricewaterhouseCoopers and the services that they offer. A pre-listening exercise focuses attention on some of the activities that the speaker mentions on the cassette. You may need to go over the answers to this section in order to make sure that students have grasped the main ideas.

KEY:

1 FAS **b** provide advice on finance
2 MCS **c** advise on performance
3 TLS **d** provide taxation advice
4 ABAS **a** check company accounts

2 Students should try to complete the exercise before listening to the cassette.

TAPESCRIPT:

Interviewer:
I wonder if you could each give us a brief description of how the departments that you work for at PricewaterhouseCoopers are organised and what different types of services they provide?

Speaker 1:
Of course, although it's not easy to summarise such a big organisation as ours without oversimplifying things a little. In my case I work in FAS, which stands for Financial Advisory Services and we provide financial advice to companies around the world. We er might be asked, for example, to give advice to a company that is considering a merger or an acquisition. Or an organisation might require our help with arranging the finance for some really large project like building a power station. Another aspect of FAS deals with what we call 'Business Recovery and Restructuring' and here we are usually working with companies that have run into financial difficulties and which need to reorganise. Lastly FAS also includes Valuations, which, as its name suggests, involves valuing businesses for companies and investors to see exactly what they are worth.

Speaker 2:
I work in MCS or Management Consulting Services and here we tend to concentrate on advising our clients about the performance side of their businesses. We do this in a variety of ways. We can help companies define their business strategy, which sets out the ways in which they intend to grow and develop the business. Sometimes we work more on the detailed day-to-day operations, looking at how to improve the ways in which a company runs its business. We also have specialists who review the clients' information technology systems and suggest how they can be improved and in some cases even managing the department for them.

Speaker 3:
Clients come to us in Tax and Legal Services, or TLS, for advice on a whole range of questions involving taxation. This could involve personal tax or business taxes such as corporation tax. Or we might be consulted about issues relating to international trade or financing a deal.

Speaker 4:
Since I joined the company, I've worked in Assurance Business Advisory Services (or ABAS for short). Here we focus on the accounting and auditing of client's businesses. In auditing, we review the financial statements of an organisation and provide an opinion on whether the figures presented are true. There is also what we call Transaction Support where we work together with clients who are involved in mergers or acquisitions to help them to get a clear picture of the accounts and business activities of a target company. Finally we also provide evaluations of global risk and help companies to manage the risks that are associated with their businesses which in turn contributes to improving both their management and performance.

KEY:

2 TLS 'issues relating to international trade'
3 FAS 'companies that have run into financial difficulties and which need to reorganise.'
4 MCS 'review the clients' information technology systems'
5 MCS 'the ways in which they intend to grow and develop the business.'
6 FAS 'Valuations, ...'
7 ABAS 'provide an opinion on whether the figures presented are true.'

3 This short introductory reading passage explains in simple terms what an annual report is. The subject is developed in greater detail in the main reading text. You may wish to bring in examples of annual reports at this stage or leave this until students have read the main text. Annual reports can usually be obtained by writing to companies directly. They are also available at the Internet sites of major companies. Examples can be found at:

US:

www.ibm.com/annualreport/
www.benjerry.com/fin/1998ar/index–f.html

UK:

www.marks–and–spencer.co.uk/corporate/annual99/
www.bae.co.uk/annual97/home.html

KEY:

1 An annual report presents and discusses a company's financial affairs to its shareholders and investors.
2 Stakeholders are everyone with a financial interest in a company, and this includes employees, suppliers, customers and lenders as well as shareholders.

Reading

This text is part of an IBM guide to help people to understand how financial information is presented in an annual report. Although this is quite a complex area of Business English, the text explains clearly and concisely exactly what types of information can be found in the different parts of an annual report. It is important to point out that this particular document deals with the required and standard sections for American listed companies. As mentioned earlier, each country has its own regulations in matters of accountancy and this also applies to how information is presented in an annual report.

1 In this short exercise ask students to scan the text quickly and fit the headings into the text.

KEY:

3 Financial statements and notes
4 Selected financial data
5 Management discussion
6 Board of directors and management
7 Stockholder information
8 Letter to stockholders
9 Corporate message
10 Financial highlights

2 Some vocabulary may present problems and students may need assistance with following: *compliance, lifeblood, adequacy, mission.*

It is also important to point out that in English we use the word *direction* (para 8, line 7) to refer to where something is headed – it is not a synonym for 'a senior management team'.

KEY:

1 Letter to stockholders (= UK shareholders)
2 Selected financial data
3 Management discussion
4 Report of management
5 Letter to stockholders (= UK shareholders)

Vocabulary

1 KEY:

2 f
3 a
4 e
5 b
6 d

2 KEY:

2 costs (expenses)
3 currency
4 deposits
5 cash equivalents
6 assets
7 liabilities
8 gross profit ('gross' is pronounced like the adjective 'close')
9 net earnings/income

3 KEY:

b costs
c gross profit
e net earnings/income

Vocabulary development: nouns and prepositions

1 KEY:

b into
c in/with
d in
e for
f with/in
g of
h on
i into/on
j on/of

2 A wide variety of words are possible.

KEY: (suggested answers only)

b an enquiry into fraud
c involvement in community affairs / with local communities
d an interest in the development of a company
e support for a project
f satisfaction with results / in completing the report
g a percentage of sales
h a tax on profits
i research into electronics / the effects of pollution
j an effect on performance / of the cutbacks

Language Focus

Fractions and percentages

This exercise provides revision of both of these areas. A short consolidation exercise follows, in which students combine fractions and percentages with adverbs of approximation.

KEY:

½	a half
⅔	two thirds
¼	one quarter
¾	three quarters
⅖	two fifths
⅚	five sixths
9/10	nine tenths

Practice

KEY:

Different meaning: roughly

2 nearly a fifth
3 roughly one eighth
4 44%
5 roughly a quarter
6 quarter / 25%

Business Skills Focus: Presentations

Listening

1 This short listening extract will familiarise students with the type of work done by analysts before the presentation section which looks at the profession in more detail. Before listening to the cassette, ask students for their views about what they think a financial analyst does. Do not confirm or reject their ideas yet. Now listen to the extract. Were students' predictions correct? Then listen again.

TAPESCRIPT:

OK. So my name's Carole Imbert and I'm a financial analyst with CPR, an investment bank in Paris. I've been working as an analyst for five years now and I have always been specialised in the same sector, the pharmaceutical sector, although I do also deal with consumer goods and cosmetics as well. There are really two main parts to my job. The first is to study individual companies and the markets in which they operate and the second is to prepare reports and to present these to investors.

For the pharmaceutical sector, I would start by saying that it is a very big sector indeed, and probably represents something like three hundred billion dollars. The increase in the sector is on average six or seven percent per annum and there is one very big market which is the US and which represents about forty percent of the total world market.

What are the main problems facing the sector? I would say that the principal problem is related to research and development because today the companies are having to invest huge amounts of money to try to find new products which, of course, is a very expensive process and when you realise that only fifteen percent of products actually make it to the market then you can understand why you need to be a very powerful business to survive. It's the main reason why we've seen so much consolidation in this sector and I'm sure that there's more to come.

As for the future, well I would say it looks good and I'm very confident about it. People are getting older and older every year and the average age is going up. And er ... when people are older they want to have a better life and also they have more money to spend to improve their lives so I think it's a very good area to invest in.

KEY:

1 c 2 b 3 c 4 b

2 Before doing this second listening exercise, it may be useful to hold a discussion on presentations. Ask students when and why people give presentations and ask for examples of the best/worst presentations that they have listened to. They can now work in pairs to prepare a list of the factors that they think contribute to making a good presentation. Two or three pairs can then present their conclusions to the rest of the class.

TAPESCRIPT:

Because students need the tapescript to focus on language items in Speaking, the full tapescript is on page 163 of the Student's Book.

KEY:

a 7 b 1 c 6 d 2 e 3 f 4 g 5

3 KEY:

listed: By 'listed' we mean that these are companies in which you and I can invest, they are open to the public ...

brokerage firms: which are really just companies specialised in buying and selling different types of financial investment.

4 Students should pay particular attention to what Carole says in this part of her talk and in particular to the actual words she uses to refer to the information that she is presenting on the transparency. This will help them when they come to make their own presentations later in the unit.

KEY:

b

5 The main purpose of this question is to encourage students to consider the differences between written and spoken English. Make clear that even if a presentation is written out, it should contain language that is appropriate to spoken discourse and which takes into account the important fact that an audience of listeners, not readers, is being addressed. There are several factors to consider when deciding whether to present from notes or from a complete text. The following table highlights the key advantages and disadvantages of each approach.

KEY:

Carole Imbert is speaking from notes.

	Speaking from notes	Speaking from text
Disadvantages	greater language fluency and memorisation needed; rehearsal usually necessary; only limited information can be written down	less personal; less eye contact; no visual check of audience understanding; risk of becoming monotonous; written and not spoken discourse
Advantages	better audience contact; own personal style; greater mobility; more 'friendly/authentic'	no hesitations; no errors with terminology; all details organised; self-assurance of a planned script; copy of full text can be distributed

Speaking

Giving a presentation

1 Using appropriate signposting language is a crucial factor in making a presentation so that an audience knows what a speaker is doing at each stage. In this exercise the four questions relate to this aspect.

If you want to review signposting in more detail, you can ask students to give examples of the language they would use for the following:

giving examples (*for example, such as, for instance*)

making comparisons (*like, compared to, more than*)

showing differences (*whereas, unlike, by contrast, on the other hand*)

asking rhetorical questions (*This isn't necessary, is it? Do you really think that …?*)

concluding (*to finish, and in conclusion*)

closing (*Are there any questions? Thanks for your attention.*)

KEY:

a *I think I will begin by … Once I've explained that, I will go on to describe … and then, to finish … After that …*

b *I suppose that the answer to that first question 'what does an analyst do'… As I said before …*

c *If you look at the transparency … At the top here … Then, next to it … Below that …*

d *I'm going to give you an example of … If we now move on to …*

2 Give students enough time to prepare their presentations. Discuss the guidelines to making a presentation in the photocopiable materials on page 81–83. This includes useful notes on voice and body language together with a list of useful expressions to use in presentations.

It may also be useful to bring in marker pens and transparencies that students may need for the overhead projector.

3 Taking notes is an important element of this exercise as students will need them to complete the writing exercise that follows. Encourage students to ask questions after the presentations and seek clarification if necessary.

Writing

Make sure students structure their reports, which should contain an introduction explaining how they have organised the information that they are presenting. There is a photocopiable sample report on page 84.

Review 2 Key

Grammar check

1

2 be processed
3 still
4 will be informed
5 will discontinue
6 Although
7 has been made
8 to be done
9 will
10 enable
11 will
12 have been tested
13 will produce
14 is given
15 Although
16 let
17 have agreed
18 Even though
19 are going to
20 will

2

2 had known ... would have increased
3 fall ... will switch
4 reduce ... will do
5 weren't ... would use
6 had bought ... would have lost
7 increase ... will expand
8 hadn't cut ... would not have survived
9 had ... would be able
10 don't deliver ... won't use/won't be using

3

2 slight decrease
3 fell / dropped
4 changed / fell / dropped
5 50%
6 rise
7 slight increase
8 7%
9 1/4
10 1/2

Vocabulary check

1

Banking	The Environment
balance	recycling
debit card	global warming
cashpoint	waste
deposit	sustainability

The Stock Market	Import Export
dividend	tariffs
issue shares	quota
broker	local subsidiary
yield	duties

Company Performance
chief financial officer
net profit
balance sheet
revenue

2

2 revenue
3 net profit
4 dividends
5 sustainability
6 waste
7 local subsidiaries
8 quotas
9 to issue shares
10 chief financial officer

3

2 with
3 out
4 off
5 for
6 of
7 into
8 off
9 on
10 out

unit 11

Setting Up a Business

Key vocabulary

This section explains the different types of business organisations that exist in the UK and gives the equivalent forms for the US. One way of leading into the subject is to ask students if they have any idea of how businesses can be set up in their countries. From this general discussion you can explain the notions of *liability* and *share capital* which are central features of the different types of business organisations. The terms *unlimited* or *limited liability* indicate that the owners of a business either have, or do not have, responsibility for the repayment of debts. It should be pointed out that limited liability generally concerns only Private and Public Limited companies (UK) or open and close corporations (US) whereas other forms of business organisation usually involve unlimited liability. It may be necessary to explain that the term *share capital* refers to the proportion of shares of capital that individual investors provide. There is a photocopiable exercise on page 71 to check students understand crucial terms related to business organisation.

Public limited companies (UK) or **close corporations** (US)
As students will already have studied the stock exchange and company performance, they will know that companies can only be listed on the markets after they have satisfied the conditions imposed by the relevant government regulatory authority. In the UK only companies that have been registered as plc's can trade their shares on the open market. The procedures for registering a plc are very similar to those required for a Ltd except that the minimum share capital is much higher.

Sole Trader (UK) or **Sole Proprietor** (US and UK)
It should be explained that this is the easiest way of setting up a business (no legal formalities, no disclosure of accounts and no business taxation). For these reasons it is well suited to small-sized operations such as small shops.

Partnership
Mention that with this form of business it is almost always necessary to draw up a formal partnership agreement in which the procedures for running the business, the precise roles of each partner and the proportion of shares are defined.

Private limited companies (UK) or **open corporations** (US)
Although this is the most common form of business in the UK, students should understand that when setting up a company of this type, specific administrative procedures must be followed which usually require specialist legal advice. Before a limited company can be officially registered, two important documents have to be drawn up: the memorandum of association, and the articles of association. The first of these documents contains the details concerning the company's share capital and its commercial objectives, and the second lays out rules for the internal management of the company.

Lead-in

1 This section checks that students have grasped the differences between the various arrangements for starting a business, and that they understand the implications that these differences have on the way the business is managed and can develop.

KEY:

Advantages
1 a sole trader
2 a partnership
3 a private limited company
4 a private limited company

Disadvantages
1 a partnership
2 a partnership / sole trader
3 a partnership / sole trader

As a follow-up, students can discuss private limited companies and suggest advantages, such as access to capital markets or greater recognition, and disadvantages, such as administrative complexity or regulation.

2 This brainstorming activity encourages students to come up with essential questions that need to be considered in the early stages of preparing a business project. It will help them to appreciate difficulties entrepreneurs have to face in setting up businesses, and will familiarise them with some of the basic vocabulary they will have to use later in this unit.

Students first make a list of questions in pairs. Get them to group their questions under these headings: *finance, product, recruitment, market, organisation.* Following this, a selection of questions from the different pairs can be put on the board and discussed. Many questions are possible and some examples are given below:

Finance

How much money will I need?

What collateral (security as a guarantee for the money) do I have?

What are my profit expectations?

Where will I get it from?

Product

Which suppliers will I use?

What equipment, if any, do I need for production?

How will I package my product?

What quantities of stock will I need to hold?

Where will I stock my products?

How will I distribute my product?

Recruitment

How many employees will I need to have?

What skills or experience do I need?

Where will I find suitable employees?

What will be my employment policy?

Market

Is there a market for what I want to sell?

Who do I want to sell to?

What is the competition like in this sector?

How much can I charge?

How will I promote my product?

Organisation

What arrangement for the business would be best?

What type of premises do I need?

Will my needs change, for example what is the implication of growth potential?

Where should I locate the business?

Reading

1 Most students should be familiar with both the major computer manufacturers such as IBM, Apple, Compaq, Sun, etc., and also the main software producers like Microsoft, Netscape, Novell, Lotus, etc.

KEY:

1 This is a general question and can be a class discussion.
2 Students may have problems identifying the photos of the entrepreneurs:

1 f Apricot	3 b Apple
2 d Microsoft	4 a Sun

2 The text gives a profile of Roger Foster and traces his career through the different businesses that he has set up. Students may also have difficulties with the following vocabulary and idiomatic expressions:

Vocabulary: *cumbersome* (para 3) *flopped* (para 10) *sortie* (para 10) *profit warnings* (para 14) *infighting* (para 14) *brainchild* (para 16)

Idiomatic expressions: *the next big wave* (para 2) *the light dawned* (para 3) *let the advantage slip* (para 9) *proved fatal* (para 11) *got the timing wrong* (para 11) *the next wave to catch* (para 13) *was in trouble* (para 14) *was paralysed by* (para 14) *stepped in* (para 15) *to slot together* (para 16) *as far as the eye can see* (para 19)

KEY:

2 a	**3 c**	**4 d**	**5 e**
6 b	**7 f**	**8 g**	**9 h**

3 KEY:

a offering computer programming to corporate customers; distributing PCs; making PCs; being the first software company to be listed; creating specialist business software components that can be fitted together
b seeing the future of microprocessors and creating the Apricot; identifying the market for financial software and buying relevant companies
c launching Apricot in the US against Apple; failing to switch to IBM-compatible computing; infighting in the boardroom

Vocabulary

1 KEY:

2 computer programming	5 launch
3 distributing	6 restructuring
4 manufacturing	

2 KEY:

2 c	4 b	6 h	8 g
3 f	5 d	7 a	

3 You may want to introduce this short exercise by asking students to imagine how a company selling beer could use the Internet to help it to develop its business. Although students will suggest marketing and advertising and perhaps e-commerce, they probably will not see how a company can use the Internet as a source of funding for start-up companies.

KEY:

2 advantage	5 predicts
3 ventures	6 demand
4 entrepreneurs	7 industry

Vocabulary development: prefixes

1 These exercises continue the focus on separable prefixes introduced in Unit 5. It is important to point out that these prefixes carry secondary stress and that they are often not hyphenated (except *co-* and *ex-*).

KEY:

2 b	4 c	6 d
3 f	5 a	

2 KEY:

b postdate; predate	f postgraduate
c prearranged	g interpersonal
d international; multinational	h ex-husband
e ex-director	i biannual

3 KEY: (suggested answers only)

1 inter: active, city, departmental, face, net, racial, section, weave

2 post: natal, mortem, script, war
3 bi: centenary, cycle, focal, lateral, monthly, partisan, weekly
4 pre: cooked, fix, heat, marital, mature, meditated, natal, recorded
5 multi: coloured, cultural, lateral, millionaire, national, purpose, storey
6 ex: boss, chairperson, partner, wife

Language Focus

Relative clauses

This is an area students often have problems with. This section provides a review of relative clauses and consolidation exercises on defining and non-defining relative clauses. Encourage students to look at the Grammar Reference material on page 168 of the Student's Book.

KEY:

1 A 2 B

Practice

1 KEY:

2 N	4 D	6 D
3 N	5 N	

2 KEY:

1 This is one of the videos (**which / that**) we use for training purposes.
2 Have you read the report (**which / that**) I left on your desk last night?
3 The candidates (**who(m) / that**) we interviewed were very highly qualified.
4 What's the name of the secretary **whose** computer crashed last week?
5 The woman **who** introduced me to Mr Ross was Australian.

We can omit the relative pronoun from sentences 1, 2 and 3 – it refers to the object of the sentence mentioned in the first clause (1: 'the videos', 2: 'the report', 3: 'The candidates').

3 KEY:

2 e	4 b	6 a
3 f	5 g	7 d

Skills Focus

Speaking

You may want to begin with a short brainstorm on the qualities needed to be a successful businessperson and then individual students can decide whether they want to be an entrepreneur. Attention can now turn to the questionnaire. Explain that it has been adapted from those used by various banks to help their customers to consider whether they have the qualities and skills that are necessary to run a business. Although the vocabulary in it is for the most part relatively simple, you may need to explain some words and expressions, such as: *to get on with someone, self-starter, to be willing, to cope with, to foresee*. You may want to discuss which quality each question is evaluating. Students then complete the questionnaire. Make it clear to students that they should not see this questionnaire merely as a character test, but rather as an opportunity for self-assessment of their potential as entrepreneurs. It is a pointless exercise unless they give honest answers that best reflect how they evaluate themselves as entrepreneurs. They should not choose answers that they think will get the highest score.

When they have completed the questionnaire, students can discuss their results in pairs. Following this, you may wish to discuss whether they think this type of questionnaire and the scoring system gives a realistic analysis.

Listening

This interview shows how a complex new concept was developed into a successful business venture.

1 Students should be able to guess the order in which these different things were done. However, it may not necessarily be the same as the one that was actually used in the project. For instance, stages **e** and **g** could easily be inverted. The stages are identified in the tapescript below.

KEY:

a 4	**d** 8	**g** 5
b 3	**e** 7	**h** 6
c 2	**f** 1	

2 TAPESCRIPT:

Interviewer:
How did the idea for this company emerge?

Spokesman:
I suppose the project really started as a result of a study that was made by the VDMA, that is the association of German Mechanical and Plant Manufacturers.

Interviewer:
What was so significant about this study?

Spokesman:
Well basically it revealed the existence of a new market in cargo transport because it showed that a large number of major firms in the world have enormous problems when they need to move heavy or large objects from one place to another over relatively long distances. The more remote the destination the more complicated and expensive it gets.

Interviewer:
In other words you identified the market?

Spokesman:
Yes absolutely. We knew more or less what the requirements of these companies were, the dimensions and weights of what they needed to transport, and were able to calculate the approximate size of the market.

Interviewer:
So what was the concept behind the Cargolifter? What original solutions were you proposing?

Spokesman:
Our idea was to use an airship to do the job of lifting heavy units and transporting them over long distances.

Interviewer:
What was the first step in getting the project running?

Spokesman:
Well the first thing we had to find out was if the idea would actually work! So we put together a team of engineers from different fields like transport, science and construction engineering and we asked them to do a feasibility study, to look at all the problems that would be involved both in designing the airship itself but also in building it. When that was done then we knew that we had a project that could really work.

Interviewer:
So where did you go from there?

Spokesman:
Well the next stage was to set up the company, find the money we needed and start planning the development of the whole project. With a big project like this you need a lot of money for research and for investment in facilities.

Interviewer:
How did you put together the financing of Cargolifter?

Spokesman:
We decided to raise venture capital and find investors who would be willing to take the risk. In fact initially we invited private investors, who now make up more than 60% of our shareholders. Then we sought the support of the big firms from the transport and construction and engineering sectors like ABB and Siemens and they joined the project as shareholders. Finally, we contacted smaller companies in cargo transport to see if they would be interested in joining us.

Interviewer:
So where is the project at today?

Spokesman:
Well we're in the process of building our production unit on an airfield in Brandenburg. And we're still on course to have our first ship, the Cargolifter CL 160 flying in a year from now. Then we plan to develop bigger versions in the future.

Writing

1 You may want to link the writing activity by stating that we examined earlier how larger companies go about setting up as a business. Students now have an opportunity to write a plan for an imaginary business of their own. This section provides them with a checklist of the types of information that business plans normally include.

KEY:

a 8	**d** 4	**g** 5
b 1	**e** 6	**h** 3
c 7	**f** 2	

It may also be helpful at this stage to refer back to the list of suggested questions in the Lead-in 2 activity.

2 Although this is presented as a writing activity, it is quite possible to extend it for further speaking practice by having each group of students give an oral summary of their ideas for a new business. This can be done once the writing assignment has been completed. Alternatively, you may wish to organise a role-play with groups working in pairs: Group A presents its project and Group B represents the bank. Each group then switches roles.

Another possibility is to form a panel with one representative from each group. The panel then assesses the different business proposals presented to it by each of the original groups and chooses any it would support.

You could finish the activity with a general discussion of the projects and the assessments.

unit 12

Corporate Alliances and Acquisitions

Key vocabulary

This section provides simple definitions of the different types of corporate deals or contracts made in the business world today. Before students read through these explanations, you may want to introduce the topic by asking questions which lead students to produce the vocabulary themselves. Alternatively, you may wish to ask students to close their books and fill the gaps in the photocopiable exercise on page 71 after listening to the cassette version. The following is a list of possible questions together with possible answers:

1 What options are open to businesses when they are competing with each other in the same market, if they want to avoid a price war? (Answer: Co-operate on pricing policies./Form a merger.)

2 What is one of the most expensive areas of investment (after salaries) in, for example, the automobile or the pharmaceutical industries? (Answer: Research & Development)

3 Can you suggest a way to reduce the high costs of Research & Development? (Answer: Form a merger with another company in the same line of business and share R&D costs. or: Set up a joint venture project to do the R&D for the two companies.)

4 What should a big successful company do if a smaller one produces cheaper and/or better quality products? (Answer: Buy them out, in other words make an acquisition.)

5 What advantages can be gained by co-operating with another firm when purchasing raw materials or components? (Answer: Bulk buying means economies of scale.)

6 (This question should generate the answer to question 7) How have businessmen in Western Europe reacted to the opening up of the East European markets? (Answer: They have been buying up businesses there/setting up joint ventures.)

7 Can you think of any recent corporate alliances? (Answer: students will probably mention the automobile alliances.)

8 Have you ever read about a failed merger or corporate alliance, and why did it fail? (This question is optional since it will depend on the type of student.)

These questions will encourage students to think about the present business environment and should lead them into discussion about co-operation between businesses in general and specifically about cost sharing in areas such as R&D and purchasing. Students should also be encouraged to talk about why some business deals do not go through.

Lead-in

1 This exercise gives students an opportunity to check if they have understood fully the differences between mergers, joint ventures and acquisitions. Ask the pairs of students to read the text and underline the words which told them the answers.

KEY:

1 **a** are discussing a deal that would combine …
2 **a** This business project will be owned by EIAZ and GM …
3 **c** call off talks on the sale of newstand chain Ruch …
4 **b** planning to work together …form one bigger and stronger bank …
5 **c** had agreed a deal to buy …

2 The purpose of this short pre-listening extract is to get students thinking and talking about why mergers fail (the theme of the main reading text in this Unit). As an introduction, ask students if they know anything about the merger of Volvo and Renault.

KEY:

1 F 2 T 3 T 4 F

TAPESCRIPT:

Journalist:
Ms Galfard, the last time we spoke, you explained to me in detail what was going to be involved in the Renault–Volvo merger, which at that time had already been announced and looked very much like it was going ahead. Could you speak to me today about why that merger failed?

Ms Galfard:
As a matter of fact, it is a little bit complicated to give you one short answer but I'll try to be as brief as possible. The reasons are varied and I think personally that nobody knows the exact reason for the failure. First, there are typically Swedish reasons. Many shareholders, and in particular small shareholders, were worried about what would happen to this Swedish company which they considered to be more or less a national symbol, and they were afraid that the French company would take over, so they were not in favour of the alliance.

Then, of course, you had complications with some of the managers, who believed that it wasn't going to be as good for business as they had originally hoped, and they made an official statement of their fears and advised that the merger should not go further. So, there was a board meeting at the beginning of December 1993, and during this board meeting it was decided not to go ahead with the merger. Then the

CEO, Mr Gyllenhammer, walked out of that meeting and later resigned. So, Volvo developed a new strategy with a new management team in April of the following year.

3 In pairs, students discuss reasons why mergers fail. They may come up with suggestions such as: difficulties to agree on costs/prices, refusal of one company to reduce staff, lack of trust in management personalities. The whole class can then contribute reasons which can be listed on the board. To prepare them for reading the text, it might be useful at this stage to ask the class questions such as: When a merger takes place between two companies how do they decide who will be the CEO? Do both CEOs run the new structure together? How easy do you think it would be for CEOs to share power? What kinds of people make good CEOs? etc.

Reading

1 The text describes the contribution managers' egos can make to failed mergers. There are few vocabulary issues, but students may have problems with the following (others will be dealt with in the exercises for this section):

Vocabulary: *power-hungry* (line 38) *scenarios* (100)

Idiomatic expressions: *jungle* (title) *a textbook example* (lines 9–10) *beasts of the jungle* (line 24) *boardroom bust-up* (line 42) *tie the knot* (line 65) *added spice to* (lines 77–78)

Refer students to the list of reasons why mergers fail. Ask them to now read the text once to see if it mentions any of the suggestions on their list.

2 KEY: (suggested answers only)

1 This alliance would have brought considerable financial advantages to both companies and would have made them the leader in their sector. It would have increased their R & D budgets.
2 The deal did not go through because the CEOs of the companies failed to agree.
3 Nicholas Bates explains that many senior business people find it difficult to get along with their peers because they have such strong and sometimes almost 'psycho-pathological ' personalities.
4 The author points out that the Ciba-Sandoz merger worked because senior personnel were either ready for retirement or willing to give up their posts for other ones.
5 A successful merger is possible if CEOs are willing to make the necessary compromises to bring about the most advantages for their shareholders. This means that CEOs must put the company's interests before their personal desires for power.

Vocabulary

1 This is a straightforward check on understanding vocabulary items but begins to introduce a focus on metaphor.

KEY:

2 c 4 a 6 c 8 a
3 a 5 c 7 b

2 This exercise is designed to get students thinking about the use of metaphor in English. You may want to ask students to suggest other examples associated with marriage. These could include: *turn somebody down, a long engagement* (sometimes used to describe the long negotiations that take place before a merger), *be left standing at the altar* (used to describe a company's failure to convince another one to make an alliance deal) and *honeymoon* (used to describe a period of mutual understanding and confidence).

KEY:

bust-up, to tie the knot, marriage plans

3 Encourage students to talk in pairs about the images these idioms create. Then they can look at them in context and try to guess what each one means.

KEY: (suggested answers only)

1 To combat, to fight with (perhaps suggesting a childish fight), to try to stop the other one from advancing
2 To become the boss of a company, to be the number one in a particular company
3 A serious disagreement, or ending of a business relationship between directors of the board
4 To be in charge
5 To accept playing a less prominent role, to take a less direct or hands-on role

Vocabulary development: phrasal verbs 2

These exercises focus on phrasal verbs which are also featured in Units 8 and Unit 15.

1 This is a quick check on identifying transitive and intransitive phrasal verbs.

KEY:

1 b 2 a

2 KEY:

b ended up e getting on h go by
c stand down f go under
d speak up g look ahead

Discussion

Before starting the discussion work, you may need to read through the text checking important or difficult vocabulary such as *commandeers meetings, bold, tight deadline, trappings* and *on the go*.

Whether certain characteristics are useful or not depends on personal opinion. Encourage students to discuss their differences of opinion. For example, some students may consider an impressive office and secretaries to be essential because they can impress clients. Others may consider these things to be a waste of company money. Likewise, trips on Concorde are sometimes important in order to avoid jet lag but some students will consider this far too extravagant. However, it is likely that all students will agree that being competitive about drinking alcohol is dangerous and not listening to the opinion of others at meetings is counter-productive.

Language Focus

Modal verbs of obligation

This section focuses on modal verbs which most students will have problems with, especially the difference between *mustn't* and *needn't*. You may need to explain what 'obligation' means, and give examples of modal verbs used to express obligation, mild obligation and no obligation. For additional information, refer students to the Grammar Reference material on pages 168-9 of the Student's Book.

KEY:

2 b	**4** c	**6** a	**8** c
3 b	**5** c	**7** a	

To consolidate and prepare for the next practice, ask students to produce a few sentences of their own using these modals verbs in sentences. It may be more productive to emphasise *advice* can be a synonym for *mild obligation*, in other words they may prefer to write sentences in the form of advice, such as *You need to ...* .

Practice

This practice focuses on modals verbs related to obligation, an important area for business and link with the text used in the earlier discussion. You may want to check understanding by asking students to explain what some of their answers mean.

KEY: (suggested answers only)

He needs to stop dominating conversations / interrupting others, etc.

He mustn't think he's always right / be so impatient.

He doesn't need to be so competitive.

He ought to be more patient / more considerate when others are speaking.

He should stop trying to be the centre of attention at parties / try to relax more.

He doesn't have to sleep much but he should stop liking tight deadlines.

He must get more sleep.

Business Skills Focus: Meetings

Listening

The previous exercises will have prepared students for this recorded advice from a management consultant. Before playing the tape, you should point out that this is a listening dictation and therefore they must take notes and not try to fill in the blanks of exercise 2 at this point. There is quite a lot of information missing for some of the blanks and it simply would not fit, even in note form, in the Student's Book. An appropriate procedure is to play the tape once, then a second time during which students take notes. You may want students to then discuss possible answers in pairs before they write out the missing phrases.

KEY/TAPESCRIPT:

If a meeting is to be productive, it should have [1]**a clear and stated purpose** that all the participants know and understand. You should appoint a [2]**chairperson** who manages and controls the meeting.

You must write an [3]**agenda**, or list of items to be discussed and send it [4]**to all the people concerned**. They should [5]**prepare for the meeting** and come to it with ideas to contribute.

You have to [6]**attach a time limit** to each point, otherwise there is a risk that some of the items will not be dealt with at all.

You ought to [7]**limit the meeting to 90 minutes**. If not, you have to [8]**schedule breaks** into the agenda.

You don't need to [9]**invite all the important staff members to every meeting**. But you should send other senior staff members [10]**the minutes**, or summary of what was discussed.

The minutes should include [11]**a clear summary of the important points** – you don't have to [12]**include everything that was said at the meeting**. However, you need to include [13]**actions** decided upon at the meeting. Lastly, the minutes should [14]**be sent within twenty-four hours.** It is essential to keep the [15]**meeting's results and future actions** clear in everyone's mind.

Speaking

1 This first step in the speaking activity is to familiarise students with the language they will need to use in the role-play that follows. They are asked to read the roles of the chairperson and participants and then match the expressions to each role. Some expressions may be used in both roles. A key is provided below but it should be pointed out that the chairperson may also need to use expressions of agreement and disagreement in a meeting. Some 'inappropriate' expressions have been added to the list. You may want to initiate a short discussion on the issue of register in business discussions. 'Inappropriate' expressions, though probably regularly used in heated discussion during meetings, are best avoided if a meeting is to be entirely successful.

KEY:

1 h
2 b g
3 g b
4 a
5 i
6 f c
7 e
8 f
9 d
10 h j

2 As you can see from the key, several of the expressions can be put in more than one of the categories.

KEY:

1 c i
2 e h
3 b d
4 f l
5 k g
6 a j

3 Encourage students to brainstorm other expressions they may know using some of the topics listed in **a – m** above. They may also suggest 'inappropriate' informal expressions such as *no way*, *forget it*, *Are you out of your mind?* etc. Ask each time whether the group considers these appropriate and why / why not.

Role-play

Before you start the role-play, you may want encourage a short discussion about the advantages and disadvantages of working a 35-hour week from the different points of view of various people working in a company. It may also be useful to check that students understand the role-play by asking some questions, for example about the various roles in a meeting or constraints such as time.

1 Photocopy the material on page 85. This includes useful notes, expressions to use in a business meeting and instructions about timing. The actual task is divided into steps. First, students should read the text carefully. Ask them to take notes on the feelings and opinions expressed concerning the 35-hour week.

2 Divide students into groups and assign roles to the members of each group. It would probably be best to assign the role of chairperson to a student with a good level of English in each group. Give students five to ten minutes to read the agenda and their role. They may need to ask some vocabulary questions at this stage. Then, allow a further ten to fifteen minutes to prepare notes for the meeting. Students can discuss suitable expressions, for example using modal verbs to express advice or obligation, or expressions of agreement and disagreement in their groups at this stage. You may prefer to allow students from each group with the same roles to meet and prepare their role before they split up for the role-plays.

3 Groups now conduct their meetings following the agenda closely, including the timing. Make sure that all students contribute and that the language is being used correctly. Remind them to take notes for the final writing stage of this activity.

Writing

Students now write up the minutes of the meeting using the content and order of the agenda in the Student's Book. You can use the photocopiable model on page 86. This written work may be done in class or given as a homework assignment. You may want to compare the different sets of minutes and discuss outcomes.

Marketing

Key vocabulary

This section provides an explanation of marketing and explains the four main aspects of the marketing process: 'the four Ps'. Before reading the text in the Student's Book (which is also on tape) ask students to compare definitions of 'marketing' from a learner's dictionary such as the *New Longman Dictionary of Business English*:

> marketing activities intended to make and attract a profitable demand for a product by means such as advertising, sales promotion, pricing, etc.

and from a specialist textbook such as Kotler's *Principles of Marketing* (Prentice Hall):

> 'a social and managerial process by which individuals and groups obtain what they need and want through creating and exchanging products and value with others.'

Now write 'P' four times on the board and ask students to come up with the four elements themselves. Most full-time business students will have studied 'the four Ps' in a marketing class in their own language and will easily guess how they translate into English. The photocopiable exercise on page 72 offers an opportunity to check that students understand what 'the four Ps' are.

Lead-in

1 In the previous unit students looked at marriage metaphors in business. This exercise considers military metaphors which are often used in texts about marketing. Before listening to the cassette, brainstorm with students expressions used in business which include military terms. These include '*aggressive* advertising', 'a sales *campaign*', 'staff *casualties*' 'a marketing *strategy*', 'strongarm *tactics*' etc. Encourage students to think of actual examples such as 'the cola *war*' (Pepsi/Coke), 'the sportswear *war*' (Nike/Reebok) or 'the burger *war*' (McDonald's/Burger King).

You may want students to read the text and try to guess items for the gaps before listening. Students should then listen to the tape as often as they need to find the missing words and expressions.

TAPESCRIPT:

Marketing is the term given to all the different activities intended to make and attract a profitable demand for a product. This involves:

- identifying consumer needs and wants in order to develop the product.
- setting the price.
- deciding on the best place to sell the product.
- deciding on how best to promote the product.

These four factors are often referred to as 'The Four Ps' or the 'marketing mix'.

KEY:

1 sales strategy
2 Losses
3 country
4 main markets
5 cannot compete
6 give up
7 marketing plan
8 continue

2 Make sure students understand the military expressions in the box. Then, working in pairs, they should replace the words and expressions 1–8 from the previous exercise with an appropriate military metaphor from the box. Point out that although it may not be necessary to reproduce this language in an oral context, it is essential to understand military metaphor in order to understand fully most texts about marketing.

KEY:

1 campaign
2 Casualties
3 territory
4 key strongholds
5 are outgunned
6 surrender
7 surprise attack
8 rage on

3 Students work in pairs to list ways of conducting market research. This could be 'primary' data (information for a particular project) or 'secondary' data (collected for many purposes and often used as a starting-point). They will certainly know methods for 'primary' data such as the interview in the street/shopping centre method. They may also think of telephone surveys. Newspapers and magazines ask subscribers to fill in questionnaires about their publications and they usually offer a free copy or similar gift to the people who accept. Handing out free samples and asking consumers to write back with their comments or giving them a follow-up phone call, is also popular for certain products. Sources for 'secondary' data can include statistics, company reports, articles in journals, official information, etc.

Reading

The text describes a marketing research project used to identify buying habits. There are very few vocabulary issues (the Student Book notes UK/US differences such as *petrol/gasoline*), but some of the following items may also need explaining:

Vocabulary: *hassle-free* (introductory paragraph) *anthropological* (para 5) *control orientated* (para 6)

Idiomatic expressions: *a fragmented market* (para 1) *cutting edge research* (para 2) *the common thread* (para 7) *ahead of the game* (para 8)

1 The exercise focuses attention on marketing methods and links with the previous exercise.

KEY:

Answers to this exercise will depend on the outcomes from Lead-in 3 above. Reading the text, students will identify the techniques used by Shell: they interviewed 55,000 people in 45-minute interviews in shopping centres. They then had the results of these interviews analysed by expert psychologists and defined their market in terms of customer segments. The marketing people then 'moved in' with customers to observe them fully and get a better understanding of the market.

2 This exercise is intended to confirm that students have understood the text fully.

KEY:

a 4
b 5
c 1
d 8
e 3
f 7
g 2
h 6

3 You will want to link this text to their earlier focus on 'the four P's'. Ask students questions to identify 'the four P's' and also to show how these are usually adapted to fit a particular context, for example 'product' is often adapted to 'service'. Suitable questions are: What product or service do Shell Oil want to sell? What is their pricing policy? How do Shell Oil get their product to the customer? How do Shell Oil inform, persuade or influence their target markets?

KEY:

Product	Price	Place	Promotion
good quality fuel	competitive price	nearby location	a new brand initiative
fast pumps		hassle-free fuelling and buying	new advertising campaign
quick payment			
clear instructions		quicker and easier service	
system upgrades		comfort	
		safety	
new operating practices		quick access	
simple transactions			
monitoring system			

Vocabulary

1 This exercise checks that students understand vocabulary which is common in marketing contexts.

KEY:

2 d
3 c
4 a
5 b
6 h
7 e
8 f

2 This exercise focuses on compounds related to marketing.

KEY:

2 cutting edge
3 buying decisions
4 focus group
5 common thread
6 measurement system

3 Finally, students have an opportunity to use the vocabulary in another setting.

KEY:

2 profiles
3 fragmented markets
4 determine
5 buying decisions
6 audience
7 monitor

Vocabulary development: compound adjectives 2

These exercises continue the focus on compound adjectives introduced in Unit 9.

1 As a check on understanding, ask students how quickly they can find a compound adjective in the text. You may want to reverse tasks 1 and 2 by asking students how many combinations are possible using words from A with B.

KEY:

b overpriced
c downmarket
d understaffed
e outdated
f overworked
g updated
h underpaid
i overdrawn

2 You may have already completed this task. After the lists have been produced, encourage students to check meanings for any unfamiliar compounds in a dictionary. You may want to use this opportunity to talk briefly about the notion of collocation – words that can occur together – reminding students that there are no rules and often no logical reason why some combinations are possible and others are not.

KEY:

overstaffed, overpaid, underpriced.

Discussion

to tie the knot,These three questions are designed to get students thinking and talking about market research. Allow students some time to prepare their ideas for each question in pairs and then open the discussion with the class as a whole.

2 KEY:

1 The target profile for this advertisement is the 'premium speeders' segment of the market. Ask students to justify their answer. You may want to ask them whether they think it is a good way to appeal to that particular target and why.
2 Students are asked to come up with some ideas for possible advertisements for the other two segments identified by the Shell marketing people. Encourage them to think carefully about the customer profile and to consider the type of advertisement which would appeal to them.

Language Focus

Comparison

Students often make mistakes with comparisons and they are often used in business contexts; it is therefore worth focusing on. You may want to start by reminding students that most one-syllable and a few two-syllable adjectives form the comparison by adding *(e)r* and *(e)st*, and longer adjectives use *more/less* and *(the) most/least*. There are several words and phrases students can use to say things are similar or different and by how much, including *(not) as ... as ..., as many/few as ... or as much/little as ..., (not) the same (as ...), like ...* There are also several words and phrases (called quantifiers) we can use in front of adjectives which express degrees of difference. You may want to refer students to the examples in the Student's Book and brainstorm others before students complete the exercise in class or for homework. For additional information, refer students to the Grammar Reference material on page 169 of the Student's Book.

KEY:

a *a small degree of difference*	b *a degree of difference*	c *a large degree of difference*
slightly	moderately	considerably
a little	somewhat	significantly
		much
		far

Practice

KEY:

1 This year's sales figures are slightly / a little higher than last year.
2 Advertising to children has become somewhat / moderately easier.
3 Our products are a little / slightly more expensive than our competitors'.
4 Advertising laws in Europe are far / considerably / much / significantly more complicated.
5 This year's market share is slightly / a little better.
6 English is considerably / significantly / far more useful than other languages for business.

Reported speech

You may want to remind students that we can report statements, questions and thoughts and we can choose from many reporting verbs such as *say, ask, think, believe, suggest, explain.* Brainstorm others. When we use reported speech, we change personal pronouns, etc. which make the reference clear. We may also change words about place: *'I like working here'* becomes *'He said he liked working there.'* We also make changes to tenses and words about time: *'I will arrive tomorrow'* becomes *'She promised she would be arriving today.'* Because we usually report what was said in the past, we normally use a past tense for the report verb.

Practice

1 KEY:

Direct speech	Reported speech	Examples
Present simple	Past simple	1 'Where do you work?' → He asked me where I worked.
Present continuous	**Past continuous**	2 'We're expanding rapidly.' → She said they were expanding rapidly.
Past simple	Past perfect	3 'Prices went up in 1999.' → He said that prices had gone up in 1999.
Present perfect	**Past perfect**	4 'Have you finished the report?' → She asked if I had finished the report.
Future	would	5 'I'll probably be late.' → She said she would probably be late.
can	**could**	6 'I can't afford it.' → He said that he couldn't afford it.

2 KEY:

1 She said she didn't always buy the same shampoo.
2 She said the price influenced her decision most.
3 She said she had been using her present brand for two years.

4 She said she had used the previous brand for three years.
5 She said she had never used hair colour.
6 She said she liked her natural colour.
7 She said she would use hair colour if it were as easy to use as shampoo to use.
8 She said she would be willing to pay £5.
9 She said she would accept the free sample.
10 She said we couldn't phone her next week.

Skills Focus

Reading

1 This Skills Focus section gives students an insight into direct mail marketing. Students are first asked to read the description of what a good marketing letter contains. They are then asked to match the extracts to two customer profiles. Students will need to read these extracts carefully and get this first exercise right in order to complete the examples of direct mail marketing letters that follow.

KEY:

a 1	d 1	g 1
b 2	e 2	
c 1	f 2	

2 The successful completion of this exercise will depend on suitable rephrasing and ordering of the correct letter extracts on page 132 of the Student's Book.

KEY:

2 a	4 g	6 e
3 d	5 f	7 b

3 To prepare students for the writing task which follows, students should now analyse the completed letters using the criteria given at the start of this Skills Focus section. Encourage students to study the letters point by point. Elicit from them how the writer personalised the letters, ensured that the reader continues to read, etc.

Writing

1 Working in small groups, students complete the target profile for the letter they are going to write. Each group member should first complete the profile him/herself and then compare it with the other members of the group. The group can then establish one profile based on these. Some suggestions for additional headings might include: cosmetics, presents for friends and CDs. In the second part of this exercise, groups make a list of convincing arguments which will appeal to the target profile. Ask them to try to imagine how someone with the target's lifestyle would react to each of their arguments and why.

There is a photocopiable model of a letter on page 87.

2 Each student should write their letter. This may be given as a homework assignment or used as a 'writing workshop' in class, with you providing help and advice when necessary. Circulate the letters around the class and discuss which ones are best and why.

You may want to suggest an alternative writing task for homework in which students can make use of the military metaphors they focused on earlier in the unit. For example, they could prepare a written report on the marketing expectations of this direct mail campaign. Encourage them to also make use of comparisons.

unit 14

Product and Corporate Advertising

Key vocabulary

Illustrate the key vocabulary with examples of both product and corporate advertising. Show students examples of product advertisements in magazines and elicit the word *advertisement* from them. Explain that we say *an advertisement* and not ~~*an advertising*~~. Ensure that students understand the difference in meaning and pronunciation of the words *'advertise, 'advertiser, 'advertising* and *ad'vertisement*.

You may wish to use the photocopiable vocabulary exercise on page 72 to check that students understand the crucial terms.

To illustrate corporate advertising, you could use either a job offer which gives information about the company and their policies or a similar one to the BP corporate advertisement on page 141 of the Student's Book. Ask students to think of methods of communication companies use to make their policy and attitudes known to the public. These can include company websites, annual reports, newspaper articles and sponsorship of international or local sport and cultural events. Explain that these are designed to generate positive publicity about the company. If students have problems understanding the difference between *publicity* and *advertising*, point out that some publicity can be negative as we cannot always control what people will say or write about a company (although some consider that all publicity is good publicity, and you may want to mention Benetton's advertising campaign briefly at this stage – using controversial images which deliberately draw a great deal of public criticism. An example of a major company destroyed by bad publicity in the UK is Ratner's, the high street jewellery chain – its founder spoke openly about the poor quality of its cheaper products and the company collapsed as a result of the backlash). Give an example of negative publicity such as if a Boeing plane crashes, the company's name will be headline news in every newspaper and news programme. Advertising is ordered and paid for by a company and its aim is always to increase sales by creating positive attitudes towards the products being advertised.

Lead-in

1 The purpose of this section is to get students to think about different advertising media. Groups can brainstorm ways that companies advertise their products and services. These include a wide variety of print, broadcast media (TV, radio and the cinema), outdoor advertising (posters, hoardings [billboards], displays of logos at stadiums and on clothes, and skywriting), transportation advertising (racing cars, and signs on public transport vehicles and stations), point of sale advertising (window displays, product demonstrations and stands in supermarkets), websites and sales through e-commerce, and other printed media (carrier bags, calendars, matchbooks, pens, etc.). Gather together the various ideas on the board.

2 Use this discussion activity to encourage students to think about the latest trends in advertising such as free advertisements from Internet providers and virtual advertising. Encourage them to talk about their favourite ads and advertising methods. Discuss whether they find the four methods mentioned appealing or not. Ask them to think about other innovative ways to advertise such as small screens at petrol pumps at filling stations.

3 These activities are designed to have fun with slogans. You may want to display various slogans and ask students to discuss and select the best. It might be fun to ask students to translate some of them into their own languages and discuss the results. They will no doubt discover the difficulties in translating humour and word-plays, so often found in slogans.

1 The examples in the text are taken from the Internet and should provoke a discussion on the problems of international or global advertising. Ask students to read the examples and say how they would react to products bearing these slogans.

2 Students now work in groups to translate popular slogans in their language into English. They may also wish to invent new slogans in English for products. To help them, it might be productive to circulate magazines or suggest topic areas such as chocolates, beer, sportswear, perfume and shampoo.

4 This discussion task is designed to get students to talk about provocative and sometimes offensive advertising. As a preparation for the reading text, it may also be useful to ask them if they think this example from Benetton has the same affect on all age groups, or whether certain generations find it more acceptable than others, and why. You may want to include another example such as French Connection's use of FCUK on casual clothes and hoardings in Britain aimed at their young adult market.

Reading

The text examines controversial advertising. Some of the following vocabulary items may need explaining:

Vocabulary: *scraping off* (para 1) *fundamental values of society* (para 3) *retract* (para 3) *adland thinkers* (para 4) *It's all very well ... but* (para 5) *broadminded* (para 9) *shattering of taboos* (para 9)

Idiomatic expressions: *confessed to their sins* (para 3) *prostitute* (para 5) *pitching for business* (para 6)

1 When students have finished reading the text, encourage them to discuss it in the light of the example given in Lead-in 4. Ask them to describe differences between their reactions to the Benetton ad and the Volkswagen one.

2 Ask students to underline extracts in the text to justify their answers.

KEY:

2 b　3 c　4 c　5 b

Vocabulary

1 KEY:

2 posters
3 social issues
4 clients
5 pitch for business
6 coverage
7 Creative Director
8 taboo

2 KEY:

2 target
3 billboards
4 Creative Director
5 corporate image
6 publicity

Vocabulary development: uses of *like*

1 As preparation, you may want to ask students to look up *like* in a dictionary and note the wide variety of meanings and uses. Draw their attention to *like* as a verb (*I like her* = She is nice), preposition (*She looks like her mother* = She's similar to her mother), and as a plural noun (*She has her likes and dislikes* = She knows what she likes and doesn't like). Other uses of the word *like* include *unlike* and *likewise*.

KEY:

b D　c B　d A

2 KEY:

2 likened to
3 like
4 look like

Students now contribute other meanings and uses as a class discussion. Encourage them to use *like* in a sentence when they make their contributions.

Discussion

Draw students' attention to the fact that the article they have just read is an example of the type of publicity the campaign got. Remind them of earlier focuses on positive and negative publicity. Ask them whether they think this article could have a damaging or positive affect on the company's image in the short or long term.

Language Focus

Gerund and infinitive

The use of *-ing* forms and infinitives is an important area since they often occur in English structures. Explain that *-ing* forms include both participles and gerunds. Remind students that particular verbs in English can be followed by an infinitive (*agree, hope, plan*, etc.) while others use a gerund (*be, enjoy, finish*, etc.). You may want to also remind students that gerunds are always used after verb + preposition (*succeed in increasing sales*) and infinitive forms are not possible here.

KEY:

1 gerund, because 'include' is always followed by a gerund
2 *to*-infinitive, because 'decide' is always followed by an infinitive
3 A

Practice

Before doing this exercise, find out what students know about Coca-Cola. Where did it start? What was its product range? What image do the Coca-Cola commercials give of the product and the people who buy it? This exercise could be done for homework.

KEY:

A
2 to make
3 to build / building
4 transforming
5 setting up
6 to bring

B
7 to reflect
8 Creating
9 deciding
10 to appear

C
11 launching
12 changing
13 returning
14 drinking
15 to expand

The article

1 As an introduction to the focus on the use of articles, this activity encourages students to analyse a corporate advertisement. Encourage them to discuss what they learn about the company from the ad, for example that BP is a world-famous company which supplies solar energy equipment to remote parts of the world.

Point out the positive language used, such as *power, constant* and *sun* – it is intended that the reader automatically associates these words and images with BP.

Students will be led to the conclusion that the company is trying to project a caring, responsible and forward-looking image. Encourage students to look at the Grammar Reference material on page 170 of the Student's Book.

2 Ask students to underline the words in the text. You may want them to work in small groups to provide the explanations. After completing the task, students can read through the text and find other examples.

KEY:

1 power (no article) an uncountable noun when used to refer to energy
2 world (the) the definite article is always used when we refer to the planet earth
3 electricity (no article) articles are never used between adjectives and nouns
4 sun (the) the definite article is always used when we refer to the earth's star
5 needs (no article) articles are not used between adjectives and nouns. In this case needs refers to the general category and not to a specific one. Otherwise it would, be 'the local needs'.
6 difficulty (no article) an uncountable noun which refers to a general category.
7 range (a) a singular countable noun referred to for the first time
8 living standards (no article) a plural noun referring to a general category and not a specific one

Practice

As an introduction to this practice exercise, ask students what they know about the mineral water company Perrier. To guide students, ask them questions like 'What image does the product have?' 'What image crisis did they have to face in the past?' Note: Benzene is a substance obtained from petroleum and coal tar, often used to make plastics and cleaning materials. You may want students to explain their answers.

KEY:

2	a	**12**	the
3	The	**13**	The
4	A	**14**	no article
5	the	**15**	no article
6	a	**16**	no article or 'the' are both possible here, depending on whether the term 'consumers' is considered to refer to a specific group (Perrier consumers) or is being used in a wider sense (consumers in general)
7	a		
8	a		
9	a		
10	An		
11	an		

After students have completed this exercise and presented their answers, conclude by asking them how Perrier dealt with the problem and what students think of the solution.

Skills Focus

Listening

Designing a television commercial

The introductory reading passage to this listening task provides students with key audio visual terms. Read through the passage with students making sure they understand all the highlighted words. If possible, illustrate this activity by showing videos of examples of commercials which use the dramatisation technique. Ask them to describe the story after viewing each one. Alternatively, describe examples of narratives and series which use the same characters (Kenco coffee, Oxo, Tesco's, PG Tips, etc).

1 Point out that these photographs (referred to as 'stills' in audio visual terms) are a selection taken from the complete commercial. Allow them five to ten minutes to discuss the four questions.

2 Students are not asked to complete any specific task during the first listening. They are asked to concentrate on the description being given and then compare it with their own ideas. You may need to play the tape a few times.

TAPESCRIPT:

The sequence starts with a view of a handsome young man galloping across a beautiful American desert landscape in glorious sunshine. As the camera moves back we see that he is heading at full speed towards the edge of a very steep cliff. The horse stops suddenly just at the edge, which causes the rider to plunge over its shoulders into the abyss. There follows a series of different camera angles to show the man's dramatic fall from various perspectives.

Fortunately, there are a few branches growing out of the sheer rock face and our hero manages to catch onto one of them and we next see him on the right of the screen, hanging safely from it. Suddenly he begins to smile charmingly, and the camera moves left to reveal why. A beautiful young girl who has met with the same fate is hanging from another branch just opposite his!

At this moment the voice-over says 'Because you never know when you will meet the girl of your dreams, Gillette has created continuous protection anti-perspirants. They prevent odour before it begins, to keep you fresh all day long.' We then see the product in the foreground of the great desert landscape and the voice-over continues with the final slogan 'Gillette anti-perspirants; long-lasting protection that keeps you ready for anything.'

However, the love story is not yet over, and the next thing we see is the young man reaching over to give our heroine some flowers which just happened to be growing on his branch! She accepts with a smile but this will be a short-lived love affair because just at this moment our hero's branch begins to crack under his weight!

3 Students are asked to take notes under specific headings.

KEY:

1 **The characters:** A handsome, adventurous young man, riding a horse at high speed. He's athletic and strong and has a charming smile. A beautiful young woman.
2 **The setting:** An attractive American desert landscape in bright sunshine; a steep cliff face with strong branches growing out of it and a few flowers.
3 **The action:** A male rider tries to stop suddenly at the edge of a cliff and falls over the edge. He is saved by a branch and meets a young woman who has met with the same fate. He smiles at her and offers her some flowers. Suddenly, the man's branch breaks...
4 **The camera positions:** The camera starts by concentrating on the young rider and moves back to reveal the danger in store. Many different camera positions are used to show the dramatic fall. It then shows only the man but soon moves back to reveal the woman opposite him.
5 **The final slogan:** The first slogan is 'Because you never know when you will meet the girl of your dreams, Gillette has created continuous protection anti-perspirants. They prevent odour before it begins, to keep you fresh all day long.' The final slogan is: 'Gillette anti-perspirants; long-lasting protection that keeps you ready for anything.'

The tapescript uses the present simple to tell the story since the action is described as if it is happening now. The present continuous is used to describe the background in which the particular actions of the story take place.

Discussion

Students are going to create a television commercial that tells a story. Each member of the group will present one part, for example one student could say what the product and target audience are and another could explain why the group chose this particular product. Another member could then talk about the concept and ideas behind the commercial and say how they hope to appeal to the chosen target. One student could present the description, and finally another member could respond to other students' opinions of it.

Divide the class into groups and ask each group to choose a product they would like to write a scenario for. They should decide which audience or target they want to appeal to and whether they want to use humour or serious story lines. Encourage them to use a very simple story line with very few characters and give them a time limit for their ad, say 30 seconds. Ask them to make detailed descriptions of the characters in their scenario as well the action. Explain that it helps to produce a slogan and then work backwards from it. When they have chosen the slogan or central message of the commercial they can then decide how best to build up to it.

Writing

The groups of students can now write a full description of their scenario using the headings from Listening 3 to help them. Suggest they prepare a text similar to the tapescript they heard. Go around the groups checking vocabulary and making sure the correct tense is being used. One member may want to draw a rough storyboard or comic strip version to make their presentation more visual. This writing task could be omitted or given as homework.

Speaking

The groups imagine that they work for an advertising agency and have come to present their idea for an advertisement to a client. Each member of the group presents one part and then other groups express their opinions of the effectiveness of the commercial, deciding whether or not it fulfils its aim.

The Business Media

Key vocabulary

This section provides a short list of the principal types of media, and the different forms of information that they provide. You may want to introduce this Key vocabulary by bringing in examples of publications and video or audio material or you could ask students to close their books and fill the gaps in the photocopiable exercise on page 73 after listening to the cassette version. For the business press there are many specialist publications available on the market. These include weekly or monthly magazines such as *Business Week*, *Inc. Magazine*, *Fast Company*, *Forbes magazine* and *Fortune*, and also the daily newspapers like *The Wall Street Journal*, *New York Times*, *The International Herald Tribune*, or *The Financial Times*. For the broadcast media there are a number of cable and satellite channels that are either dedicated entirely to business news such as Bloomberg TV, or which feature in-depth business programmes like BBC World and CNN. Most of the providers of business information are now also present on the Internet and offer free access to certain sites such as:

www.switchboard.com www.brandsforless.com
www.hypermart.net www.bloomberg.com
www.mysteinc.com www.CNBC.com

Lead-in

This listening passage gives an introduction to the Bloomberg organisation featured in the reading text. Bloomberg provides a wide variety of media services to the business community. Four of these services are described in this interview. The task that students have to complete involves listening for general meaning rather than for specific vocabulary. They may have to listen several times to get the information. Remind them that they need to identify services/audience(s)/ media for each product, and it may be best to encourage students to note one of these three elements at a time. You may need to use the pause button.

TAPESCRIPT:

Interviewer:
What makes Bloomberg so unique in the financial services market?

Executive:
Well I think the main thing is that Bloomberg provides a broad range of services in one package. We supply not only information and analysis but also other related media products which are adapted to our customers' individual needs and requirements. 'The Bloomberg Service', our core business, provides real-time financial information, statistics and research for the markets and for businesses. This is delivered through special terminals which also show live television broadcasts prepared by our staff.

Interviewer:
Can you tell us about the media products?

Executive:
Our news service, Bloomberg News, offers complete coverage of markets, companies, politics and entertainment and is specifically designed for investors and decision-makers. This information is syndicated or sold to over 850 newspapers around the world.

Interviewer:
And Bloomberg Television?

Executive:
Well, we produce news broadcasts and programmes for our own subscribers and use them to complement other Bloomberg services. Some of these programmes are also sold to outside television networks.

Interviewer:
And what exactly is Bloomberg Personal?

Executive:
This is a magazine which is specially designed for individual investors and it offers readers investment strategies along with views and insights from top Wall Street experts.

KEY:

The Bloomberg Service
Services: Real-time financial information, statistics and live television broadcasts prepared by Bloomberg staff
Audience(s): The markets and businesses
Media: Broadcast and multimedia, using special terminals

Bloomberg News
Services: Coverage of markets, companies, politics and entertainment
Audience(s): Investors and decision-makers
Media: Print media (Press)

Bloomberg Television
Services: News broadcasts and programmes
Audience: Bloomberg subscribers
Media: Broadcast (Television)

Bloomberg Personal
Services: Investment strategies along with views and insights from top Wall Street experts
Audience: Individual investors
Media: Print (Magazine)

Reading

1 Ask students to prepare three questions about the origins, activities and future of the Bloomberg organisation. Then as a class write suggestions on the board such as *How did Michael Bloomberg get the idea for the business? Where did he get the money to open the business? How profitable is the company?*

2 Give students a time limit to read the text and answer as many of their questions as possible. You may want to review these with the whole class or just take a few sample questions from individual students. Encourage students to discuss opinions about answers to questions they still have.

3 KEY:

2 T	5 F	8 T
3 F	6 F	9 F
4 T	7 F	10 F

4 This last section provides an opportunity for students to express their reactions to the office environment in which Bloomberg employees work. Michael Bloomberg has deliberately designed his offices to bring his employees into constant contact with each other. The discussion should bring out some of the arguments for and against *open* (UK)/*cube* (US) or *closed* (UK)/*cave* (US) office layouts.

Vocabulary

The text is taken from the *New York Times* and features vocabulary studied in previous units. However, students may have difficulties with the following:

Vocabulary: *a news wire service* (lines 9–10) *cultish* (line 66) *state-of-the-art* (line 82) *utilities* (line 112) *figures* (line 122)
Idiomatic expressions: *to plaster ... on* (lines 5–6) *mask* (line 91)

1 KEY:

2 h	5 i	8 e
3 b	6 a	9 f
4 j	7 c	10 d

2 www.worldspace.com is an interesting website. Encourage students to look at it and compare the business section to the Bloomberg site.

1 KEY:

2 information	5 backing
3 broadcasts	6 subscribers
4 audiences	

Vocabulary development: phrasal verbs 3

These exercises continue the focus on phrasal verbs introduced in Units 8 and 12.

This section deals with three-part phrasal verbs and explains the different elements they are composed of. It is important to stress they are invariably transitive.

1 KEY:

b get along with	g get round to
c come in for	h miss out on
d live up to	i move over to
e go along with	j cutting back on
f get on with / get down to	

2 KEY: (suggested answers only)

go back on (change position after initially agreeing), *carry on with* (continue doing), *face up to* (confront), *check up on* (verify), *lose out on* (fail to achieve or get something), *make up for* (compensate for), *help out with* (help someone do something), *look out for* (look carefully or protect), *look down on* (consider somebody or something to be inferior), *look up to* (admire somebody)

Language Focus

could have + past participle

This section deals with how we talk about situations that were possible in the past but which did not happen. You may want to use this opportunity to deal with the other past perfect modals *should have, must have, ought to have* and *may/might have*. Encourage students to look at the Grammar Reference material on page 171 of the Student's Book.

Practice

You may want students to prepare these answers in pairs.

1 KEY: (suggested answers only)

1 He could have worked for another company.
2 He could have chosen offices in a cheaper part of London and New York.
3 He could have provided individual offices for all his staff.
4 He could have arranged to charge for catering.
5 He could have opened an office in South Africa before liberation.
6 He could have paid someone to write his life story.
7 He could have kept the money for himself.
8 He could have issued stock on the market.

2 Students should have no difficulty giving examples of things that they did and of the other options that were open to them at that time but which they did not choose to pursue. For example: *I decided to study business. I could have studied economics.*

Nouns

This exercise is designed to check students understand the complexity of noun forms and give them practice in using some of the problem nouns that occur frequently in business. Remind students of key difficulties with nouns. Nouns are either countable or uncountable and some have two or more forms with the same spelling, one of which is countable and one of which is not. Furthermore, some nouns which end in 's' are in fact singular while others have no plural 's' but are used in the plural form.

KEY:

1 a **2** c **3** b

Practice

1 KEY:

2 b	**6** c	**10** b	**14** a
3 a	**7** b	**11** c	**15** b
4 c	**8** b	**12** b	**16** b
5 a	**9** a	**13** b	

Skills Focus

This activity brings together different skills that students have worked on throughout the course and gives them an opportunity to use these in the preparation and delivery of a radio broadcast.

Listening

For a successful outcome of the broadcast role-play, it is important that students pay careful attention to this listening section as this sets the tone for the type of writing that radio bulletins require. It also shows students how to make a general introduction and how to manage the transitions between the different parts of their broadcast.

KEY:

c, a, b

TAPESCRIPT:

You're tuned to EBW the European business network. It's 5pm GMT on Monday the 28th of December and this is Colin Jeffars with the round-up of the day's main stories and financial updates plus the latest in sports news and weather. With only three days to go before the January 1st deadline, Europe moves closer to monetary union and businesses across the continent are scrambling for the switch to the new currency. Prospects of a take-over in the European pharmaceuticals industry still seem likely despite the announcement by the French luxury goods company LVMH that it has withdrawn from talks with the French drug-maker Sanofi SA. Rupert Murdoch is about to gain his long awaited entry into the Italian pay-television market and is said to be close to signing a deal with Telecom Italia that will give his company, News Corp., control of the Stream television channel. And in the aftermath of the Asian crisis, the Japanese and Hong Kong exchanges continue their downward spiral while both the Dow Jones and Nasdaq advance in early trading in New York. In London and Frankfurt values were unchanged. Now with the details on the first of those stories, here is Manfred Klarsfeld, our Brussels correspondent.

These days Europe is a divided community. On one side; the euro believers, convinced that the new currency will bring benefits to all, and on the other, the euro heretics, who see the move as yet another erosion of national identity. However for the business community there is no time for nostalgia: like it or not, the euro is here to stay. Although the euro will not be immediately available in the form of bills and coins, 11 countries will start using the common currency as of January 1st. For currency traders, bankers and major retailers this is hardly a surprise. As one London trader puts it...

Reading

Bring enough copies of articles for each group of students, or use the photocopiable articles on pages 88–91. Select articles on topics covered in the course. The level of your students will determine how long and how difficult these articles should be. Divide students into groups. Ideally provide each member of a group with an article that nobody else has in order to ensure that groups will not be duplicating reports. If you have only a limited number of articles available, make sure there are enough to provide the basis for one complete broadcast. If enough articles have been made available and if time allows, each group should have the chance to present to the full class. Encourage your students to make notes about the organisation of the key points in an article, and how sequencing has been presented.

Speaking

Allow about 15 minutes for the groups to rehearse their summaries of the articles and work on the delivery. Most students will feel more at ease if they have prepared an extact written copy of their texts when they come to the role-play. However, students may want to do this activity using only notes.

Writing

1 KEY:

1 f	**3** b	**5** d
2 c	**4** a	**6** e

2 Provide active support during the writing phase to make sure that each final text for a broadcast is appropriate for radio. Remind students that radio bulletins frequently use a combination of present simple and present perfect tenses to create a closer, more immediate link with the listener. Students can refer to earlier units for any extra vocabulary items and should make use of appropriate idiomatic expressions. Encourage them to vary the style of their report and include, for example, a short live interview rather than just a summary. This interview should have been planned and rehearsed at the Speaking stage above.

Role-play

If the equipment is available, students could record or video their broadcasts so others can listen/watch. Allow enough time at the end, at least ten minutes, for questions, comments and feedback from the class.

Review 3 Key

Grammar check

1

2 the
3 that
4 which
5 a
6 whose
7 setting up
8 the
9 that
10 to be
11 whose
12 to identify
13 who
14 which
15 power
16 whose
17 of signing
18 that
19 to stop
20 using

2

2 the (remove)
3 did (done)
4 informations (information)
5 as (like)
6 equipments (equipment)
7 don't have to (mustn't)
8 The (remove)
9 as (than)
10 as (like)

3

2 that they expected (expect) to be in a position to resume dividend payments next year
3 that we were (are) the people who would (will) decide the future of the organisation
4 that last year they had encountered (encountered) a number of unexpected problems
5 that these problems had resulted (resulted) in disappointing sales figures in their (our) main markets
6 that they had already started to work on improvements
7 that they were (are) going to have two main objectives in the coming year
8 that they had to (must) improve customer satisfaction
9 that they would have to (have to) innovate in new areas of business
10 that they could then re-establish our company as market leader

Vocabulary check

1

Setting up a business	Corporate Alliances
limited liability	takeover
entrepreneur	joint venture
sole trader	acquisition
partnership	merger
Marketing	**Advertising**
consumer profile	slogan
focus group	billboard
segment	Creative Director
research	commercial
The Business Media	
subscribe	
networks	
terminal	
broadcast	

2

2 networks
3 broadcasts
4 research
5 acquisitions
6 segments
7 subscribe
8 commercials
9 focus groups
10 consumer profiles

3

2 underworked
3 break down
4 international
5 bilingual
6 postgraduate
7 outdated
8 upmarket
9 catch on
10 pre-planned

Key vocabulary exercises

There is one exercise below for each unit in the Student's Book.

Unit 1 Company Structures

Complete the passage below using the appropriate word or phrases from the box.

Chairperson	Senior managers	Managing Director	Board of Directors

At the top of the company hierarchy is the 1................................, headed by the 2................................ (or president). The board is responsible for making policy decisions and for determining the company's strategy. It will usually appoint a 3................................ (or chief executive officer) who has overall responsibility for the running of the business.

4................................ or line managers head the various departments or functions within the company.

Unit 2 Recruitment

Complete the passage below using the appropriate words or phrases from the box.

letter of application	position	application form	shortlist
apply for	interview	recruit	recruitment agency
covering letter	CV	applicants	hire

When a company needs to 1................................ or employ new people, it may decide to advertise the job or 2................................ in the appointments section of a newspaper. People who are interested can then 3................................ the job by sending in a 4................................ or 5................................ and a 6................................ containing details of their education and experience. In some cases a company may prefer to do this initial selection after asking candidates to complete a standard 7................................ . The company's human resource department will then select the applications that it considers the most suitable and prepare a 8................................ of candidates or 9................................, who are invited to attend an 10................................ . Another way for a company to 11................................ is by using the services of a 12................................ (US = search firm) who will provide them with a list of suitable candidates.

Unit 3 Retailing

Complete the passage below using the appropriate words or phrases from the box.

shopping centres	**multiple retailers**	**superstores**	**department stores**
retail chains	**outlets**	**shops**	**retailing**

1................................ is the term that is used to describe the business of selling products directly to the general public or to individual consumers. Most companies in this sector sell from 2................................ or stores of varying sizes which are referred to as 3................................ . In the UK, the retail industry is dominated by large and powerful 4................................, which are organised nationally and sell a standardised selection of products. These 5................................ often specialise in a particular type of consumer product: electrical equipment, food, clothing, etc. Their outlets tend to be concentrated in 6................................ or malls (US) where customers have access to a large variety of stores in the same location.

Increasingly, large retailers are operating from out of town locations with parking facilities known as either 7................................ or hypermarkets depending on whether they occupy a surface area of more or less than 3,000 square metres.

8................................ such as Harrods in London, are large shops which sell a wide variety of products usually from a city centre location. As the name suggests, they are organised in departments, each with its own manager.

Unit 4 Franchising

Complete the passage below using the appropriate words or phrases from the box.

franchisor	**management services fee**	**franchise agreement**	**advertising fee**	**franchisee**
format	**operations manual**	**master franchisee**	**franchise fee**	

Franchising can be defined as a business system in which a company (or 1................................) sells an individual (or 2................................) the right to operate a business using the franchisor's established system or 3................................ . The franchisee is thus able to take advantage of the franchisor's brand names, reputation and experience.

As part of the contract (or 4................................) the franchisee pays an initial sum of money, known as a 5................................ to the franchisor and, in addition, agrees to pay a 6................................ in exchange for continuing advice and assistance which is usually calculated as a percentage of annual turnover. In certain cases the franchisee may also pay an 7................................ to contribute to the franchisor's annual advertising and marketing costs. It is important to understand that the franchisee also has to find the necessary capital to open the business.

Once the contract has been agreed, the franchisor provides an 8................................ which is a document containing all the information that the franchisee requires in order to manage his or her business. In some cases a franchisor may appoint a 9................................ to supervise all aspects of the development of the business inside a territory.

Unit 5 International Business Styles

Complete the passage below using the appropriate words or phrase from the box.

subordinates	hierarchy	delegate	national culture	authority

The amount of responsibility of any individual in a company depends on the position that he or she occupies in its [1]................................. . Managers, for example, are responsible for leading the people directly under them, who are called [2]................................. . To do this successfully, they must use their [3]................................., which is the right to take decisions and give orders that will allow their subordinates to reach certain objectives. Managers often [4]................................. authority. This means that employees, at lower levels of the company hierarchy can participate in decision-making. The characteristics of management often vary according to [5]................................., which can determine how managers are trained, how they lead people and how they approach their jobs.

Unit 6 Banking

Complete the passage below using the appropriate word or phrases from the box.

commercial banks	the Bank of England	clearing banks	merchant banks	branches

The banking sector in the United Kingdom is made up of a variety of different institutions which are supervised by the country's central bank, [1]................................. . This bank not only looks after both the government's finance and monetary policy but it also acts as banker to other banks. However, for the general public and many businesses, banking services are provided by the [2]................................. (also called the [3].................................) which have offices or [4]................................. throughout the country. These banks offer a wide range of banking services which include accepting deposits, making loans and managing their customers' accounts. [5]................................. on the other hand, do not deal with the public but specialise in providing services to companies or corporate customers. They are particularly active in arranging mergers and acquisitions and in advising on aspects of corporate finance.

Unit 7 Business and the Environment

Complete the passage below using the appopriate words or phrase from the box.

consumer society	environment	pollution	recycled	packaging

It is often said that we live in a [1]................................... ; we consider it important to buy products and services. Companies need to be aware of the impact of this on the [2].................................. , the natural world around us. Many companies use [3].................................. (boxes, bottles, etc.) which has been [4].................................. , that is made using old materials. [5].................................. , such as smoke in the air, can be reduced if companies use trains instead of road transport.

Unit 8 The Stock Market

Complete the passage below using the appropriate words or phrases from the box.

securities	shareholder	stock market/stock exchange	institutional investors
equities	stake	ordinary/common shares	dividends
bonds	issue shares	broker	traded

When a company needs to raise money in order to grow, it can do so on the [1].................................. (a market place for buying and selling shares) by choosing between two different options. It can decide to [2]............................... (or units of its capital) which can be bought by [3]............................... or by the general public. Although different types of shares or [4]............................... are available on the market, the most common are known as [5]............................... . When an investor buys a share, using the services of a specialist company or [6]............................... , he or she becomes a [7]............................... and owns a part of (or has a [8]............................... in) a particular company. Shareholders can make money if the company does well either by receiving [9]............................... which are paid to them as a proportion of a company's annual profits or by seeing the value of their shares increase.

Alternatively a company can borrow money from investors by issuing [10].............................. which are loans for fixed periods of time and which carry fixed interest rates. [11].............................. is the term that is used to refer to both bonds and shares. Each year billions of shares and bonds are sold or [12]............................. on the world's major Stock Exchanges in New York, London, Frankfurt and Tokyo.

Unit 9 Import Export

Complete the passage below using the appropriate words from the box.

protectionist	quota	export	import	tariff

The exchange of goods and services between different countries is referred to as international trade. Depending on what a country produces or needs, it can either [1].................................. (send goods to another country) or [2].................................. (bring in goods from another country).

A [3].................................. is a tax imposed on imported goods; whereas a [4].................................. is the maximum quantity of a product that may be admitted to a country during a certain period of time. These measures are said to be [5].................................. in that they raise the price of imported goods so that domestically produced goods will gain a price advantage.

Unit 10 Company Performance

Complete the passage below using the appropriate words or phrases from the box.

revenue	annual report	profits	losses
financial accounts	data	markets	costs

Companies need to know how they are performing in order to make plans for the future and to analyse and find solutions to the problems that they may be facing. To do this successfully, businesses require information not only about their own activities but also about the [1].................................. they operate in. Management accounts for the company provide key [2].................................. about operational efficiency, whereas [3].................................. give information about financial performance. This allows companies to know not only how much they are selling or how much [4].................................. they are receiving but also what their [5].................................. are or how much they have to pay for the different things that they need to operate their businesses. With this information companies can then calculate how much money they have made ([6]..................................) or how much they have lost ([7]..................................) during a specific period. Annual accounts for listed companies, whose shares are sold on the Stock Exchange, have to be presented to the public in the form of an [8].................................. which gives detailed financial and other information about companies.

Unit 11 Setting Up a Business

Match the types of companies with their corresponding definitions.

1 Sole Trader (UK) or Sole Proprietor (US)
2 Partnership (UK)
3 Private Limited Company (UK)

a When two or more people want to start a business together they can set up a partnership and agree on how the business will be operated. All partners are responsible for the debts of the partnership and profits and losses are shared between them.

b A company can be formed with a minimum of two people becoming its shareholders. In order to establish such a company, specific administrative procedures must be followed. For example, the shareholders must appoint a director and a company secretary. If the company goes out of business, the responsibility of each shareholder is limited to the amount that they have contributed. This is known as limited liability. A private limited company has the letters Ltd. (Limited) after its name.

c This is the simplest way of starting a business. You are self-employed and entirely responsible for all aspects of the management of your business.

Unit 12 Corporate Alliances and Acquisitions

Match the types of alliances with their corresponding definitions.

1 Joint venture
2 Merger
3 Acquisition or takeover

a Two companies, often in the same industry, come together to form one company. Companies may do this for many reasons, for example, to increase market share and cut costs in certain areas, such as research and development.

b This is when one company accumulates enough of another company's shares to gain control and ownership.

c Two or more companies agree to collaborate and jointly invest in a business project. This type of deal allows the partners to combine their strengths in one specific area.

Unit 13 Marketing

Complete the passage below using the appropriate words or phrase from the box.

price	product	marketing	the four Ps	promote	place

1.................................. is the term given to all the different activities intended to make a profitable demand for a product. This involves: identifying consumer needs and wants in order to develop the 2.................................; setting the 3..................................; deciding on the best 4.................................. to sell the product; deciding on how best to 5.................................. the product.

These four factors are often referred to as 6..................................

Unit 14 Product and Corporate Advertising

Complete the passage below using the appropriate words or phrases from the box.

to target	**corporate advertising**	**publicity**	**public relations**
media	**product advertising**	**image**	

1.................................. is an important part of the marketing mix. It is used to increase sales by making the product or service known to a wider audience and by emphasising its superior qualities. A company can advertise in a variety of ways, depending on how much it wishes to spend and the size and type of audience it wishes 2................................. . The different 3.................................. for advertising include television, radio, newspapers, magazines, the Internet and direct mail. The design and organisation of advertising campaigns is the job of an advertising agency.

4.................................. is not directly concerned with increasing sales of products or services but more with the overall 5.................................. a company wants to present to the public. 6.................................. experts specialise in organising actions and events which generate positive 7.................................. for companies. Original advertising campaigns can sometimes also get some extra publicity for the company by way of newspaper articles and/or TV and radio reports about the campaign.

Unit 15 The Business Media

Complete the passage below using the appropriate words from the box.

audiences	**print media**	**channels or stations**	**data**	**media**
networks	**multimedia**	**broadcasts**	**press**	**news**

The business community relies on various [1].................................. to provide information, [2]................................ and [3].................................. to its members. The [4].................................., which include newspapers, books and magazines, supply this in written form through the [5].................................. and publishing companies. Radio and television [6].................................. produce and distribute audio and audio-visual programmes or [7].................................. which cover the main events and developments in business. Recently there has been considerable expansion of [8].................................. businesses which now provide integrated media services containing sound, pictures and text to [9].................................. around the world which can be accessed through [10].................................. such as the Internet.

Unit 3 – Writing model

Retailing Questionnaire Report

'Books Unlimited' commissioned us to conduct a survey to obtain information about customer profiles, customer satisfaction with the products and services currently being offered, together with customer attitudes towards mail order and electronic commerce.

A questionnaire comprising 40 questions was prepared, tested and then used in a series of interviews with customers who were approached as they left the store. Each interview took approximately 20 minutes to complete.

After analysis of the information provided it was possible to draw the following conclusions:

Customer Profile

The vast majority of respondents (80%) were regular customers and lived within a five kilometre radius of the store. They were from a variety of professional and social backgrounds – 50% were married professionals with comfortable incomes while 25% were students from the local schools and colleges. Taking an average across the group, each customer visited the store at least two times every month spending between 10 and 100 pounds on each occasion. For the most part they had discovered the store through word of mouth although some had also heard about it through advertising on local radio or through the local press. A minority (15%) had already visited one of the company's other stores.

Customer Satisfaction

The responses showed that while customers are mostly satisfied with the level of service offered and the range of products on sale, they have some reservations both concerning the prices of certain items and the quality of the communication. Several respondents thought that the store should provide a more friendly environment to make it easier for customers to relax and browse. One respondent even suggested that a coffee and snack bar should be added for this purpose. It was pointed out that there is no seating available, that access through the main door is difficult and space in several of the aisles is too limited. Although most respondents liked the style of the window display and approved of the store's policy of accompanying new books with stickers featuring comments about authors and their works, some did feel that this was sometimes taken too far and they did not think that it should be the store's responsibility to 'judge' authors and their works. Almost everybody wanted more information to be made available in the form of either weekly newsletters or bulletins that could be picked up at the store and several wanted to know if it would be possible to have more frequent author presentations.

Customer attitudes

Approximately 50% of the respondents had already had some experience of buying books through mail order and had belonged to a book club or similar organisation. However, they felt that this was not a substitute for visiting a book store and being able to seek expert advice before purchasing a publication. Although most people were aware that it is now possible to buy books through the Internet, only a small minority (5%) had actually done so. This group cited price, availability and range of titles as being their principal motivation for buying in this way. It seems that e-commerce is still not perceived as a viable alternative to purchasing books.

Unit 5 – Lesson material

International Business Styles

Many managers agree that an understanding of cultural differences is essential when doing business abroad. The following case studies illustrate what can happen if businesspeople do not take into account the culture of the countries they are dealing with.

In groups, read the following descriptions of problems managers had when doing business abroad. Choose one and discuss what you think caused the misunderstanding. Present your interpretation of the problem to see if the rest of the class agrees with it. Could these situations cause conflict or misunderstandings in your country?

1 Mr Byrd was an ex-State Department employee hired by a well-known multinational corporation to be its 'man in Riyadh', Saudi Arabia. This retired American diplomat went to the home of a Saudi, Mr Fouad, to try to interest him in participating in a local joint venture with his company. A middle man who knew them both had introduced them. As this was a first meeting, the men's conversation began with small talk that made Mr Byrd a little impatient. Questions such as: 'how are you doing?' 'how was your flight?' 'how is your family?' and 'how is your father?' were common. Mr Byrd, familiar with all these obligatory formalities of greeting, answered 'fine'. 'Oh, my father, yes, well, he is fine, but he is getting a little deaf. I saw him a few months ago during Christmas when we took him out of the nursing home for a few days.' From that point everything froze up. Mr Byrd's mission was completely derailed. Mr Fouad remained gracious enough but obviously was uninterested in doing any business with Mr Byrd.

2 Jim Turner was attending a conference in Lyons. This was not his first trip to France and he was pleased the French colleagues he'd met previously remembered him. One evening they invited him along for dinner and began joking about the quality of the food. That surprised him. He thought the food was really rather good and said so, expecting the discussion to continue. But to his great discomfort, they then make some joke about 'Americans and food' and changed the subject. He felt somewhat excluded and didn't know what he'd done wrong.

3 This incident was reported by a British management consultant based in Paris:
'I had taken the American CEO of a New York based consulting company to a French consulting firm in Paris. The negotiations did not go well. He hadn't been in the boardroom for more than 15 minutes before he asked them what their company's annual earnings were. Without waiting for an answer to that question, he suggested they give him an estimate of their firm's market value, as he was interested in making them an offer.

4 A businesswoman recently asked why a high-level delegation of visiting Japanese clients had not approached the breakfast buffet table she had taken such great pains to prepare. 'I'd gotten out the good china and silverware and even brought in Japanese green tea for them, but no one touched a thing!'

Unit 6 – Role-play exercise

Negotiating

You are going to work with another student using one of the role cards on page 77–78. A senior sales executive has arranged to meet the purchasing manager of a European manufacturer of electronic components to negotiate prices and delivery arrangements.

Notes

Conducting a negotiation in a foreign language is a complex activity that requires a combination of listening and speaking skills. For any negotiation to succeed, each side must not only have a clear understanding of what the other side is proposing but be able to present convincing arguments in support of their own positions. Agreements usually involve a degree of compromise with each side making concessions which are usually accompanied by conditions. The following guidelines will help you adopt the right general approach during the negotiation. A selection of words and phrases you can include at different stages of the process follows.

Listening

Adopt an active approach to listening during the role-play by maintaining eye contact and an interested expression. Use appropriate body language to show acknowledgement of what is being said (i.e. nodding, smiling). Take opportunities to summarise the arguments of the other person to confirm your understanding and ask for clarification when statements are vague or ambiguous. For negotiation to be successful both sides must have the feeling that they can trust each other. Establishing such a relationship is the first priority.

Speaking

It is important that you speak slowly and clearly and explain exactly what is involved in what you are proposing. Invite the other party to respond to your proposals by asking them for feedback.

Useful words and expressions

Opening a negotiation:
I'd like to start with …
The first thing I would like to discuss is …
It seems best to start with …

Putting forward a proposal:
What we are proposing is …
We are offering …
I think we could give you …

Agreeing with a proposal:
That's fine/OK by me …
I would accept …
That's exactly what we are looking for …

Disagreeing with, or refusing a proposal:
I'm afraid that's not exactly what I had in mind.
That's not how we see it.
I can't accept that.
That's out of the question.

Imposing conditions:
We would agree to that but only if …
We can't accept that unless …
That would be on condition that …
We would be prepared to … provided …

Asking for clarification:
Could you be more specific?
What exactly are you proposing?
Can you be more precise?

Summarising what has been said:
So, what you are saying is that …
If I've got this right, you are suggesting …
Correct me if I'm wrong but are you saying that …?
Am I right in thinking that …?

Postponing a decision or playing for time:
I'm afraid we will need more time before we can make a decision.
I don't think we can commit ourselves just yet.
I'll have to get back to you on that.

Concluding a deal:
It's a deal.
You've got yourself a deal.

The role cards

Purchasing Manager

You are Kim Bardy the Purchasing Manager for Teknotronik, a European manufacturer of a range of consumer electronics and you wish to purchase a quantity of LEDs (light emitting diodes). You have arranged to meet Dave Sullivan, a sales executive of LaserLite, an American manufacturer of LEDs, in order to discuss your order.

Details Your Production Manager has informed you that he will require different quantities of LEDs (shown in the table below) and has given you a schedule for delivery dates. He has also indicated that he will probably need to re-order both blue and white LED's in the near future.

The target prices per LED that you would be prepared to pay are shown in the table below which also shows (as 'competitor's price') the prices that your company paid six months ago for LEDs bought from Electrotec, an Asian company. However, you were not satisfied with the quality, technology, and delivery times and are not repeating your order. You realise that it may be necessary to pay more for American LEDs which feature the latest technology. You would prefer to arrange for staggered delivery of the LEDs, receiving them in batches of 10,000 per month. Delivery would be FOB and invoices would be sent monthly. Conduct the negotiation and remember that, if you reach an agreement, you would prefer to arrange payment at 45 days.

	Quantities	Delivery schedule
Blue	20,000	urgent (10k within 3 weeks)
White	30,000	within 3 months (10k within 4 weeks)
Red	50,000	quite urgent max 2 (total within 8 weeks)
Green	50,000	quite urgent max 2 (total within 12 weeks)

	Target price per LED (prices in euros, FOB)	
Blue	7 (target price)	5 (competitor's price)
White	7	5
Red	1.50	0.80
Green	7	5

Sales Executive

You are Dave Sullivan, a senior sales executive of LaserLite, an American manufacturer and importer of LEDs (light emitting diodes) and other electronic components. You have arranged to meet Kim Bardy, the Purchasing Manager of Teknotronik, a European manufacturer of electronic components. Ms Bardy has informed you that she is interested in obtaining a quote for an order of blue, white, red and green LEDs.

Details Teknotronik have given you quantities of LEDs they require (shown in a table below) together with a schedule for delivery dates. The prices that you would be prepared to sell at are set out in another table below: You will need a minimum production time of 4–6 weeks before delivery. You would also prefer to make one delivery for the total amount with an invoice for payment at 30 days. However, this is negotiable.

Conduct the negotiation with Kim Bardy. Remember that you usually offer a gesture of goodwill to new and potentially interesting customers. This could be to give a greater price quantity discount than the one corresponding to an actual order. For instance on a single order above 30k for Green LEDs you might offer to sell them at 7 euros per unit instead of the listed price of 8 euros.

	Quantities required	Delivery schedule required
Blue	20,000	urgent (10k within 3 weeks)
White	30,000	within 3 months (10k within 4 weeks)
Red	50,000	urgent (total within 8 weeks)
Green	50,000	urgent (total within 12 weeks)

Prices per LED (prices in euros, FOB)

	Quantity			
	(0–1k)	(1–10k)	(10–30k)	(30k +)
Blue	14	12	10	8
White	14	12	10	8
Red	n.a.	1.50	1.0	0.90
Green	14	12	10	8

The role cards

The Chairperson

Study the language of chairing a meeting carefully and be ready to fulfil your role as the organiser of the meeting. Prepare a short introduction about the benefits of performance-related pay.

You must convince the participants that it is a positive move for your company, and develop some arguments to this effect, for example:

- Increased competition leads to an increase in efficiency.
- It discourages absenteeism.
- It has a motivating effect.
- It provides an opportunity to reward individual achievement.

You will accept some of the compromise suggestions put forward and delegate the organisation of these 'action points' to the relevant people.

Fix a date and time for the next meeting to discuss progress on agreed action points.

The Human Resource Manager

Opinions

You have mixed feelings about this proposal and are undecided. Among other things, it will mean an increased workload for your department. You feel that very clear specifications need to be drawn up re-grading performance goals, and you are very concerned about assessment methods.

Suggestions

A series of meetings with the other managers to decide on a systematic method of establishing objectives as well as clear criteria for evaluation.

Attitude

Open to opinions and suggestions which will help you decide.

The Trade Union Representative

Opinions

You strongly disagree. You are particularly concerned about an unhealthy emphasis on individual achievement. You feel that the senior reliable and steady workers will earn less than their younger and more dynamic counterparts.

Suggestions

You would reluctantly accept an evaluation of teams and teamwork rather than individual performance and would favour giving 'team supervisor' titles to older members of the factory staff.

Attitude

You will insist on obtaining the above conditions before negotiating with the workers on behalf of the management.

The Production Manager

Opinions

You are very much against this proposal. You feel it will create an over-competitive attitude and have a counterproductive effect on output.

Suggestions

You would reluctantly accept a trial period of, say, six months with a guarantee that the idea will definitely be dropped if the trial proves unsuccessful.

Attitude

You stand firm on your opinion but you would accept a reasonable compromise if the Trade Union representative thinks it will be acceptable to the workers.

The Sales Manager

Opinions

You think it is an excellent idea. You've been working successfully with a 'bonus for good performance' scheme with the sales people for the last five years. The Chairperson knows your opinion, has already asked for your support and expects you to help him/her convince the others of the benefits.

Suggestions

You would be willing to collaborate closely with the Human Resources Manager on the best methods of putting performance-related pay into practice at all levels of the company. You advocate using the services of a consultant who specialises in the application of this method of payment into companies such as yours.

Attitudes

You are strongly opposed to the opinion of people who won't accept innovation and change, and you will argue firmly for what you see as a positive move for the company.

Writing the Minutes

Using the notes you took at the meeting, write up the Minutes. Remember the Minutes of a meeting should include:

- a summary of the Chairperson's introduction
- a summary of the opinions and suggestions made by the participants
- the action points that were decided upon
- the people responsible for carrying out the action points
- the deadlines that were fixed
- the date and time of the next meeting

There is a photocopiable model set of Minutes on page 86.

Unit 7 – Writing model

Letter asking for Sponsorship

PEOPLE IN NEED
P O BOX 103 LONDON NE2 5CR

Dear Ms Hayden,

I am a member of a team in charge of fundraising for the well-known and popular charity in our town 'People in Need'. We are currently working on a new action which will provide a hot meal service to old and disabled people in the area. We feel sure that you will welcome an opportunity to support such a deserving and important cause.

The first delivery of hot meals is programmed for Christmas week. The local press has already agreed to give us extensive media coverage and is especially interested in profiling sponsor companies. We have two vans at our disposal and we intend to feature sponsors' names on these too. If you agree to become part of this project, it will be of no surprise to the people of our town. Since setting up here, you have been much admired for your work in the community. Your customers, staff and shareholders have become accustomed to seeing your name connected with charitable causes such as ours. Indeed many of the people who will benefit from our new service are in fact relatives of your present staff and actual or potential customers.

We therefore feel confident that you will want to contribute to the success of our project. Our team are at your disposal to discuss the particulars with you in detail. Please do not hesitate to contact us for further details or to make an appointment.

Looking forward to hearing from you soon.

Yours sincerely,

Margaret Powell

Ms M Powell
Project Supervisor

Stock Market Articles and Summaries

Sony loss weakens profit

SONY CORP. has announced disappointing results which include both a general decline in annual profit for the year and an unexpected loss for the final quarter. In percentage terms the corporation's profit performance was down by almost 20% compared to last year. Increased costs and slow moving electronic goods were the main factors behind the drop in profit. However, on a more positive note, Sony confirmed the spectacular performance of its new PlayStation which has prevented profit levels from slipping further. Meanwhile, the company continues to reorganise its main business activities as it moves into promising new sectors such as networking. Sony's share prices have risen by 35% during the last two months as investors have regained confidence in the company's long-term potential.

Summary and effect on share prices

The Sony Corporation has had problems during the last year as a result of lower sales and higher costs. As a result they have announced lower profit figures for the year. The company continues to produce highly successful products such as the Playstation and is expanding into new areas of business. The poor results have not brought down the share prices which have actually increased in recent months as investors believe that the company remains an attractive investment.

Drug company down on revised sales

MCKESSON HBOC INC., North America's leading drug wholesaler, has officially announced a downward revision of almost 5% to its declared annual earnings. The move accompanies an admission that the sales figures for its newly-acquired software business were incorrectly recorded. Following the announcement, the company's shares lost $31 to finish at $34.75 reducing the market value of McKesson by $8 billion. A company spokesman revealed that further revisions may be necessary as it continues its investigation into software sales during the previous quarters.

Summary and effect on share prices

The shares of McKesson HBOC Inc. fell sharply in value following an announcement that there were some inaccuracies in the figures for the sales of software products. These errors meant that the company had to reduce the earnings per share and its market value declined.

US success story

DaimlerChrysler is riding the wave of the strong US economy as profit and revenue in the automobile industry continues to increase. The company announced a 23% increase in profit for the first quarter with a net profit of 1.6 billion euros ($1.7 billion). Revenue is also up 10% to 53 billion euros. A company spokesman said 'We are selling what people want.'

This strong first quarter suggests that the company will surpass its target for the coming financial year. The future for American car manufacturers looks good.

Summary and effect on share prices

DaimlerChrysler is doing well as the US demand for cars continues to rise.

As a result, share prices are rising and shareholders may expect higher dividends. It is reasonable to expect that share prices will continue to increase as the forecast for the coming financial year is very good.

Unit 10 – Presentation exercise

Making a presentation

You are going to make a presentation about the Canadian company Bombadier Inc. using the information in the charts and tables on pages 82-83.

Notes

Making a presentation in a foreign language is a complex task and represents a challenge that can be a stressful experience, especially if you have never given a presentation before. These guidelines contain invaluable advice about all aspects of presenting, and include appropriate language to use in order to signpost your talk clearly so that your audience can follow the transitions between the different sections.

Voice

The audience must be able to hear and understand what you are saying. Speakers tend to speak too softly, too fast and without pausing or varying the tone of voice. You can practise by speaking about something you know or have an opinion about. Pay careful attention to when you include pauses, volume changes and variations in tone of voice.

Body Language

Adopting the right body position and using appropriate gestures to show interest, highlight points, and keep your audience's attention are important factors. Address your audience as 'you' as this helps to make both sides feel closer and makes you more relaxed. Remember:

- Make eye contact with the audience, turning your head so that you regularly look at every member of the audience.
- Move around a little if you are standing, and vary the position of your upper body if you are sitting down. Use your hands and arms to provide gestures at appropriate moments.

Useful words and expressions

Using appropriate words and phrases at key moments of a talk makes it easier for your audience to follow what you **are** saying and to anticipate what you **will be** saying next. This list will help you to highlight the key stages and to indicate the transitions between the different sections of your talk.

Introducing the talk:
This morning I'm going to be talking about …
In my talk today I will be looking at …
I'd like to start by giving you …

Indicating the structure and sequences of your talk:
I have divided my presentation into X sections …
In the first section I will / am going to describe …
Then I will / am going to go on to …
After that I will / am going to look at …
Finally I will / am going to …

Moving from one section of your talk to another:
I would now like to go on to the next point which is …
If I can now move on to the next section …
To continue …

Summarising and condensing what you have said:
To recap …
The main thing/s to remember is / are …
The point that I am making here is that …

Highlighting:
This is particularly important because …
I can't stress enough that …
It should be pointed out that …
I would like to draw your attention to …

Giving examples:
For instance …
For example …
such as …
like …
A case in point is …
i.e. (pronounced 'eye' and 'ee' as in 'see')

Inviting questions and feedback from the audience:
Are there any questions so far?
Feel free to ask if you have any questions.
I welcome questions if at any point you don't understand something.
If you have any questions about this, please/do ask.

Asking rhetorical questions (questions that the audience are not expected to answer):
Some of you may be wondering how can this be done?
Am I right in thinking that …?
So, just how can this be achieved?
You may be wondering how long will this take?

Referring to information on an overhead:
If you have a look at this figure here …
As you can see from the table …
This particular slide shows …

Drawing conclusions:
This means that …
Consequently …
As a result …
Therefore …

Closing your talk:
I would just like to finish by saying …
To finish I would just like to remind you …
In conclusion, thank you …
Do you have any questions?

The Charts and Tables

Figure 1 *Bombardier at a glance*

Bombardier

Bombardier Transportation	Bombardier Recreational Products	Bombardier Aerospace	Bombardier Capital	Bombardier International
Passenger Rail Vehicles	Snowmobiles	Regional Aircraft	Commercial and Industrial Finance	
Transportation Systems	Watercraft and Sport Boats	Business Aircraft	Mortgage Finance	
Operations and Maintenance	Engines	Amphibious Aircraft	Consumer Finance	
Freight Wagons	Neighborhood Vehicles	Defence Services	Inventory Finance	
	All-Terrain Vehicles		Technology Management and Finance	
	Utility Vehicles		International Finance	

Figure 2 *Bombardier Number of Employees as at January 31,1999*

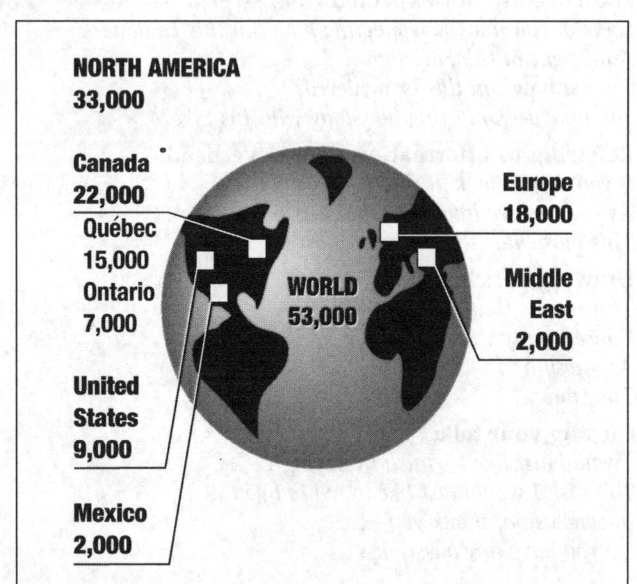

Figure 3 *Bombardier Revenues by Industry Segments as at January 31, 1999 (millions of Canadian dollars)*

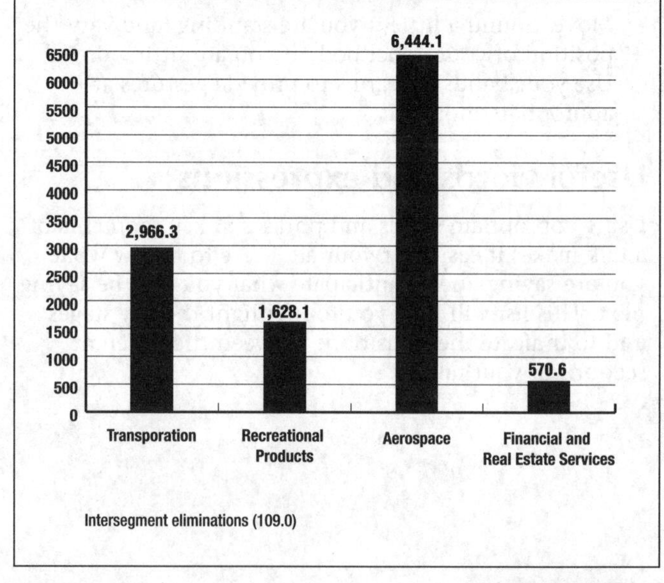

Figure 4 *Bombardier Highlights*

Highlights

(millions of Canadian dollars, except per share amounts)

For the years ended January 31	1999	1998
Revenues	$ 11,500.1	$ 8,508.9
Income before income taxes	$ 826.9	$ 627.2
Income taxes	$ 272.9	$ 207.0
Net income	$554.0	$ 420.2
Earnings per share	$ 0.77	$ 0.59
Dividend per common share:		
Class A	$ 0.170000	$ 0.150000
Class B	$ 0.173125	$ 0.153125

As at January 31	1999	1998
Total assets	$ 14,272.2	$ 10,575.2
Shareholders' equity	$ 3,488.5	$ 2,889.3
Additions to fixed assets	$ 364.2	$ 262.6
Backlog	$ 25,510.9	$ 18,104.1
Book value per common share	$ 4.40	$ 3.57
Number of common shares	683,172,995	678,918.448
Shareholders of record	10,097	10,781

Figure 5 *5 year revenues*

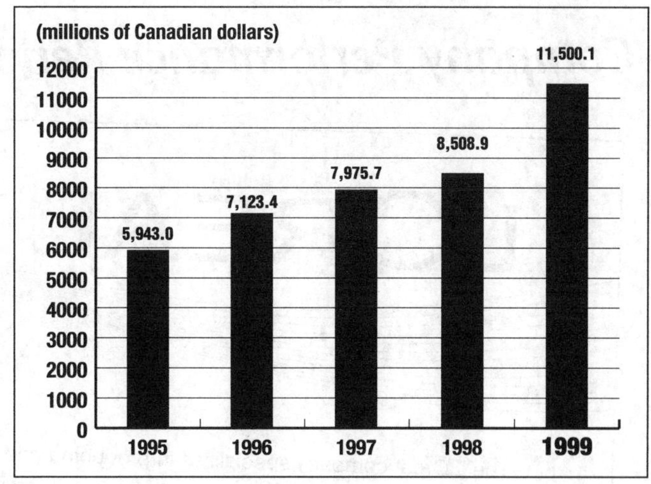

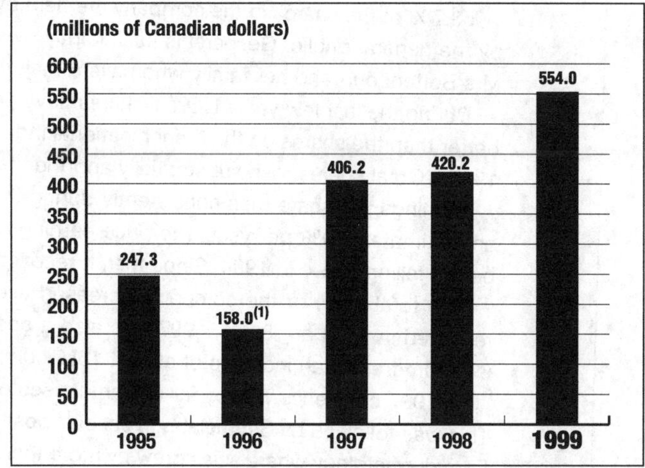

Figure 6 *5 year income*

Figure 7 *Stock performance*

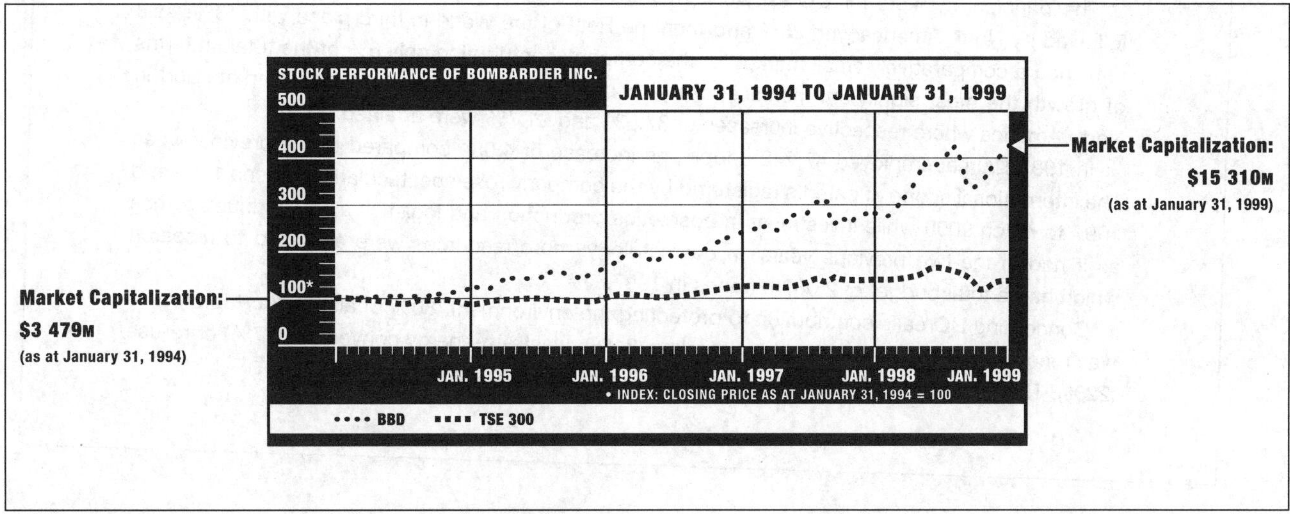

Unit 10 – Writing model

Company Performance Report

L'ORÉAL

The L'Oréal company specialises in producing and marketing cosmetics which are sold worldwide. In addition to this core business, it also has interests in 'Synthélabo', a pharmaceutical laboratory, and is active in the sector of dermatology.

53.7% of the shares in the company are held by Gesparel while the remaining 46.3% are owned by the general public. Gesparel is itself jointly owned by Nestlé which has 49% of the capital, and Mrs Bettencourt and her family who have a majority stake of 51%.

During the last few years L'Oréal shares have performed well in general terms and comparatively better than the shares on the French national index the CAC 40. Between the end of 1995 and mid-1997 L'Oréal shares rose substantially and then fell back to finish 1997 at 2400 francs.

Earnings per share rose consistently during the five-year period from 1993 to 1997 at a rate of approximately 10% per year. The price earnings ratio reached its highest point in 1992 and 1993 before falling to 1.4 in 1994. Since then it recovered to 1.8 in 1998.

The total sales of the company increased every year from 1993 to 1997 with the biggest rise recorded in 1994 at 18.6%. 1997 was also a good year for the company with sales amounting to 69,120m francs, an increase of almost 15% compared to the previous year.

In 1997 cosmetics was by far the largest sector for sales, accounting for 81.3% of total revenue. This was followed by Synthélabo in second position with 17%. The most spectacular growth came from dermatology where sales grew by more than 50%. However, this sector only represented 1.1% of total sales.

The two divisions that contributed the most to the performance in the cosmetics sector were the Consumer Division which accounted for 55.2% of sales, an 18.1% increase compared to the previous year, and the Perfumes and Beauty Division which produced 26.9% of total sales, representing a 12% improvement in performance.

The principal markets for L'Oréal were Western Europe which was in first position with 56% followed by North America with 25% and then the Rest of the World in third place with 13%. Asia remained a comparatively small market for the company contributing only 6% of the total. In terms of growth the most significant increases were recorded in the Rest of the World markets and in North America where respective increases of 37.5% and 21.7% were attained.

In 1997 L'Oréal employed 47,242 people, an increase of 4,084 compared to the previous year. The international scope of patents registered by the company rose spectacularly between 1995 and 1997 to reach 9000 while investment in cosmetics production and logistics also continued to rise as it had in the two previous years. In cosmetology, more resources were allocated to research which had a total budget of 2,089m francs in 1997.

Concerning L'Oréal's contribution to protecting the environment, 80% of all transportable waste was recovered in 1997 through either recycling (31%), waste-to-energy conversion (27%) or re-use (22%). The remaining 20% was either destroyed (3%) or disposed of in landfill (17%).

Unit 12 – Role-play exercise

A Business Meeting

You are going to participate in a business meeting to decide on the introduction of performance-related pay and you will have one of the roles described in the role cards in the Communication Activities section at the end of the Student's Book. After the meeting write a set of Minutes for which you will need to take notes.

Notes

Participating effectively in meetings is an essential skill that even experienced professionals have difficulties with. Much has been written on how to avoid totally unproductive meetings: have a clear agenda, stick to it and make sure everyone comes prepared, etc. However, the success of any meeting depends almost entirely on the personalities of the participants. Listen carefully to others, have respect for everyone's points of view and wait for your turn to speak. If you chair the meeting, be firm about focusing on the agenda or topic, keeping to the time allotted for each speaker, encouraging less outgoing people to contribute and stopping people who are dominating and/or being irrelevant.

The items on the agenda for the meeting in Unit 12 and the following role-play cover topics of general interest and no special knowledge of business is required in order to participate fully. Express your own opinions as much as possible and use the role cards as guidelines only. You will need to prepare the content of your contributions using the language items provided in Unit 12 as well as suitable expressions from the lists below.

Useful words and expressions

The chairperson

Opening the meeting and presenting the agenda:
Welcome everyone …
The purpose of this meeting is to …
Do you all have a copy of the agenda?
Perhaps we could start with the first point, which is …

Keeping things moving:
Mr/Ms X, would you like to speak now?
We'd like to hear your idea Mr/Ms X.
Let's move onto the next point.
OK, I think you've made your point so let's now consider …

Ensuring everyone stays focused and contributes:
That's not relevant, could you stick to the point please.
Mrs X, I don't think we've heard from you yet.
What do you think are the marketing/financial implications?
Does everyone follow?

Keeping an eye on time:
I'll have to ask you to be as brief as possible as we are running out of time.
I'm afraid our time is almost up.

Summarising:
To sum up …
To summarise what has been said so far …

Seeking clarification:
What exactly do you mean when you say …
Could you tell us a bit more about …
Do you mean … ?
If I understand correctly, you think …

Making sure everyone agrees on action points:
The next step is to …
Are we all agreed?
So, it seems we all agree that …

Putting people in charge of action points and establishing deadlines:
Mr X could you look after …
How soon can you get back to us on … ?
Will next Friday be OK?

Closing the meeting:
I think we've covered/that covers everything.
Thank you for participating.
The next meeting will be …

The participants

Expressing opinions:
I think/consider/feel that …
I have no doubt that …
I definitely think that …

Agreeing and disagreeing:
I agree. / Agreed.
I'm in favour of that.
I can't accept that. / I disagree.
I'm afraid I don't agree with you.
You may be right, but …

Making recommendations:
I suggest we …
I would recommend …
We should maybe …
May I suggest …

Agreeing to get involved in action points:
No problem, I'll do that right away.
I could have it done by early next week.
I don't mind doing…

Timing

The Chairperson will open the meeting and introduce the topic. (3 mins)

Each member will be invited to put forward his/her opinions and views. (5 mins per person)

A general discussion period will follow during which each member will present suggestions and recommendations to help reach a satisfactory compromise. Action points will be decided upon. (20 mins)

The Chairperson will appoint people to be responsible for various action points and then close the meeting. (5 mins)

Unit 12 – Writing model

Minutes

Here is a model set of Minutes for a business meeting.

Minutes of the meeting on Tuesday the 23rd of March:

Present: Ms Lyons (chairperson), Mr Louden (TU representative), Ms Peasley (Human Resource Manager), Mr Power (Production Manager) and Mrs Banks (Finance Manager).

Ms Lyons opened the meeting with the following points:
The proposed alliance will almost certainly go ahead.
This will be very good for the company.
The alliance will mean a 35-hour week for everyone in the company.

Mr Louden was the first to speak and put forward the following opinions:
The 35-hour week is totally unacceptable to the members of the trade union.
Loss of overtime pay on already low salaries will have a serious affect on workers' motivation level.
The consequences could be dramatic if compensation packages are not considered.

Ms Peasely agreed with Mr Louden but added that:
The future of the company seems to depend on the alliance so compromises must be found.
Executives may need training for teamwork.

Mr Power expressed strong disapproval of the 35-hour week saying:
Production deadlines will be impossible to meet.
Large numbers of new staff will have to be recruited.
The workers will suffer from low morale.
They should be allowed to earn overtime while they train new staff.

Mrs Banks was the last to speak and argued that:
The 35 hour week is a very good idea for all concerned.
The company must form the alliance at any cost as it could solve present financial difficulties and bring new customers.
Looking at the long-term outcome it could mean improved profits and eventually higher salaries for everyone in the company.

After a long discussion the following action points were decided upon:
Mr Power will calculate the number of overtime hours required in order to train new staff and submit them to Mrs Banks by the end of this week.
Mrs Banks will study the possibility of performance-related pay for motivated workers and consider the proposal of perks such as increased health benefits to compensate for loss of earnings. She will also examine the cost of continuing to pay overtime to workers while they train the new people after consultation with Mr Power. She will get back to Mr Louden by the end of next week with a concrete proposal.
Mr Louden will speak to the workers about the proposed compensation packages and see if these would be acceptable. However, he still thinks that the best way to reach consensus is to ensure salary increases in the short term. He is willing to try to convince workers to accept compromise in the short term.
Ms Peasley will look into the availability and cost of special executive training courses and will then meet with Mrs Banks to discuss the possible funding of these.

Date of next meeting – 2nd of April at 10.30 in the boardroom.

Unit 13 – Writing model

Direct Marketing Letter

Forever**After**

P O Box 48 Leeds LS 22 8MS

Dear John,

Congratulations on your new career. You must be happy to be earning some real money at last. No more tight student budgets. Time to relax and enjoy buying all those things you dreamed of but couldn't afford as a student.

Wouldn't it be awful to return to those days of watching everything you spend? Wouldn't you like a guarantee that you'll never have to worry about money again? We, at 'ForeverAfter Insurance' may have the answer.

Our company protects your future by offering a retirement plan at low cost with high returns. We don't expect you to make huge sacrifices. Just the equivalent of one less night club a month means you can look forward to the time when your dancing days are over.

Just complete the attached form and send it back to us. You'll never regret the most important financial decision you have had to make so far.

Sincerely

Steve McLoughlin

S McLoughlin
Marketing

Articles

Oil Firms, Citing Competitive Pressures, Plan Cuts Over 5 Years

BEIJING — China's two largest oil companies said on Thursday they planned to cut almost 1 million jobs over the next five years, illustrating the country's dilemma as it takes halting steps to open to foreign competition but grapples with a mounting unemployment problem.

China National Petroleum Corp. and China Petrochemical (Group) Corp. said they would cut a total of about 976,000 workers.

'China's petroleum industry faces very serious challenges today,' said Liu Yan, director at the petroleum division of China's State Administration of Petroleum and Chemicals Industries. 'Our state oil companies have many inefficient units and very high costs of operations.'

The planned job cuts come amid on-again, off-again talks on China's possible entry into the World Trade Organization. Membership in the organization would require Beijing to open markets, cut import tariffs and make companies more efficient. China's state oil companies would have to compete with sources of cheaper oil imports, and oil companies around the world are merging to slash costs.

China National Petroleum, also called CNPC, plans to slash its workforce by one third in five years, from 1.5 million workers today, said Luo Yingjun, vice president at the country's largest oil company.

China Petrochemical, known as Simopec, plans to reduce its number of workers to 714,000 from 1.19 million today. Last year the company said it would cut its staff by a quarter in the next five years.

'CNPC's most serious problem today is high costs,' Mr Luo said. 'We're cutting costs to survive and be competitive.'

'We want to cut our workforce by a third in three to five years' time,' he said. 'We can't do it too quickly, or there will be a lot of social problems.'

'The job cuts could save the company as much as 4.76 billion yuan ($575 million) a year in wages, based on an average annual wage in the industry of 10,000 yuan per worker,' Mr Li said. That figure does not take into account the cost of severance payments.

The prospect of so many job losses will add to a concern that rising unemployment could threaten China's social stability.

China's urban unemployment rate at the end of last year stood at 3.1%, unchanged from the year before, according to official statistics. But economists and analysts say the actual figure could be much higher.

The Chinese authorities are now delaying plans to completely deregulate domestic oil prices for fear that an earnings decline at state oil companies could slow the country's economic growth.

'Our plans to completely deregulate domestic oil prices will have to be delayed until next year,' Mr Liu said.

Bloomberg News

Next Travel Stop for Branson: Outer Space

By Tom Buerkle,
International Herald Tribune, May 12, 1999.

LONDON — Richard Branson, the British entrepreneur who founded Virgin Atlantic Airways and failed in his quest to circle the globe in a hot-air balloon, has set his sights on a new frontier – space.

Mr Branson has registered the name Virgin Galactic Airways as a potential brand name for space flights and held talks with Rotary Rocket Co., an American company that is trying to develop a re-usable rocket for commercial uses including tourism.

'I wouldn't want to get too carried away; it's still a matter of years,' Paul Moore, a Virgin Atlantic Airways spokesman, told Bloomberg News. 'But I think it's now a matter of when, not if.'

Lest anyone dismiss the item as a mere publicity stunt, the report comes as efforts to take tourism out of this world are intensifying. A joint study by the National Aeronautics and Space Administration and the Space Transportation Association, a private U.S. group, concluded last year that prospects for space travel and tourism were fundamentally promising. Representatives of more than two dozen companies seeking to launch a new era in vacations are expected to gather in Washington next month for the association's first conference on space tourism.

Bob Haltermann, who heads the association's space travel and tourism division, predicted that companies would begin offering suborbital flights to the general public in three to five years and orbital flights in five to ten years.

At least one U.S. company, Zeagrahm Space Voyages, has begun taking deposits for suborbital space flights at $98,000 a shot.

'There are quite a few companies out there,' said Brian Berger of Space News, a U.S. weekly.

'Some of them are crackpots, and some of them aren't. What makes Branson intriguing is, he's got capital.'

A recent survey conducted for the Space Transportation Association estimated that some 55 million Americans would be ready to pay for space travel, including 4 million willing to part with $100,000 or more for a two-week ride on a space shuttle with the amenities of a cruise liner. A contest in Japan that offered credits toward five seats on Zeagrahm flights as prizes attracted 630,000 entries.

Mr Branson's interest in space may be a logical extension for a man with a flair for adventure and self-promotion. But the news did little to excite passengers of his Virgin Rail Group, which continues to suffer from the greatest number of complaints among Britain's privatized rail companies.

'His reputation on the trains isn't good,' said John Scott, assistant secretary of Britain's Rail Users' Consultative Committee. But he acknowledges that Mr Branson's rail experience would not preclude success in space. 'He's not going to be inheriting 40-year-old rolling stock,' said Mr.

Males Boost Use of Cosmetics in Europe

John Willman, FT, June 25, 1999.

Growing use by men of skin care products, fragrances and other toiletries and a return to colour cosmetics by women have contributed to the biggest growth in sales for the European cosmetics industry since the beginning of the 1990s.

Sales of cosmetics and toiletries reached 43.7bn euros ($45bn) in the European Union last year, 6.4% up on 1997, according to Colipa, the European industry body.

Country-by-country figures provide material for those fond of national stereotypes. The French, for example, are the highest spenders per capita, buying 140 euros of cosmetics and toiletries a year, compared with an EU average of 117 euros. This puts them on a par with Americans and only slightly behind the Japanese, who are the highest spenders globally.

French consumers spend a higher proportion than the average European on perfumes, cosmetics and skin care. But they spend less than average on hair care and general toiletries such as soap, shower gels and deodorants.

Despite the unromantic view of the English, UK consumers also spend more than average at 121 euros per head a year. The British spend a higher proportion on cosmetics and toiletries but less than average on perfumes and skin care.

Germany is the biggest European cosmetics market, with sales of 9.7bn euros, which puts it third globally behind the US and Japan. But Germans spend a lower proportion on fragrances and decorative cosmetics than average and more on general toiletries.

Bottom of the league table are Portugal and Greece, spending an average of 71 euros and 88 euros a head last year. Scandinavian countries also spend less than average in the Colipa figures – which exclude only duty free sales, more important in these high indirect tax countries than elsewhere.

EU per capita spending on perfumes, cosmetics, skin and hair care products and other toiletries mirrors growth in income and has reached the same level as that on bread, says Colipa.

'Most consumers now see such purchases as an essential part of the weekly shopping basket,' says Udo Frenzel of the German Industry, who heads the Colipa taskforce that collects the data.

Growth last year was the highest since the start of the decade, when the reunification of Germany boosted sales. It was similar to the increase in the US market, which is now worth slightly less than the combined EU total.

The market is dominated by large companies such as L'Oréal of France, Unilever, Procter and Gamble and Wella of Germany. But the European cosmetics industry also includes about 2,500 small and medium-sized enterpris-

BMW says future growth depends on reviving Rover

Uta Harnischfeger FT, June 25, 1999

BMW, the German automative group, yesterday said its future growth and profitability as an independent carmaker depended on whether it could revive Rover, its loss-making UK subsidiary.

The company, which has announced a £3.3bn ($5.3bn) investment package for Rover, said sharply increased output in the UK was crucial to achieving its target of lifting total BMW production by 40% to almost 1.7m units a year.

Joachim Milberg, BMW chairman, said: 'We are not allowed to gamble since the future of BMW is at stake.'

In one of his first interviews since becoming BMW chairman, Mr Milberg stressed the German group was committed to being a multi-brand car producer with a strong presence in the mass market and the sports utility segment.

Controversy over that strategy and the future of Rover led to a management upheaval at BMW this year, prompting the resignations of Bernd Pischetsreider as chairman and his deputy, Wolf Reitzle.

Mr Milberg, who succeeded Mr Pischetsreider in February, said the group's investment in Rover 'confirmed the strategy of BMW to be a full line supplier in brands and products from the Mini to Land Rover, and from BMW to Rolls Royce'.

He also reiterated the goal of making Rover profitable within the next two years. That would help lift BMW's total return on sales from 3.3% to 4.3% over the next six years.

Excluding Rover, BMW's profit margin was 9% last year.

Mr Milberg said future margins would be enhanced by an overhaul of its corporate structure, designed to deliver savings of between DM 500 million ($265m) and DM 1bn a year.

BMW's emphasis on Rover to help lift volumes and improve margins has surprised some analysts given its mounting losses in recent years.

Of the volume targets, Mr Milberg said BMW would contribute about 800,000 vehicles a year – an increase of 14%. Rover would contribute an increase of 71%, made up of 200,000 Land Rovers, 150,000 of the new Rover 75s, 350,000 new mid-size cars and up to 150,000 Minis.

His comments coincided with new figures showing that Land Rover sales rose 29% to 71,664 units in the first five months of the year. But sales at Rover declined again as the company phased out its ageing 300, 600 and 100 models.

Last year, Rover's losses increased to DM 1.87bn as productivity and quality problems undermined consumer demand. The strong pound further aggravated the situation.

Job Protection Laws 'have little effect on unemployment'

ROBERT TAYLOR, FT, JUNE 25, 1999.

Job protection laws are having 'little or no effect on overall unemployment' in Western economies, according to the Organisation for Economic Co-operation and Development.

The OECD's annual employment outlook, published yesterday, challenges conventional wisdom, but it will reassure countries - such as France and Germany – that have tough laws restricting employers' ability to dismiss workers.

The OECD says there is 'no clear link' between employment protection laws and an expansion of numbers in temporary jobs. Instead tight regulation ensures more stable jobs, less labour turnover and fewer unemployed.

Trade union leaders will be encouraged by the conclusion that innovative and flexible working practices are more likely to be introduced by companies that work closely with unions.

Firms with works councils have 'a higher rate of taking initiatives' than those without councils, says the OECD.

The detailed analysis of the labour markets of Western industrialised countries refutes some important assumptions about employment policies of many Western governments.

The report cites 'worrying evidence' that job prospects are not improving in many industrialised countries. Although the OECD forecasts a fall of 0.2% in the unemployment rate in Europe, it also expects as many as 35 million people will remain without work in the Western industrialised world next year.

The OECD concedes that, although tighter job protection may mean fewer jobless people, those without work may stay unemployed longer.

The study accepts, that while tough employment regulation means 'lower unemployment for prime-age men' (aged 24-50), this is offset by 'tentative' evidence that it ensures higher jobless rates for young workers, prime-age women and older workers. But 'only weak evidence exists that job protection has a negative effect' on those groups.

The OECD suggests there is 'no clear evidence' that practices such as team working, job rotation and flatter management hierarchies lead to the greater use of contract workers, part-timers or temporary staff. The survey also shows that skill training of adult workers in Western economies is more extensive for those already in permanent, long-term employment than the unemployed.

Diagnostic Test

Grammar

1 (50 points)

Read the following conversations carefully. **One** word is missing in each. Write the missing word in the gap. Note that short forms such as *isn't*, *can't* etc. are each one word.

Example: How are you today?
I'm fine thank you.

1 'How long has the company .... in business?' – 'We opened in 1997.'

2 'How .... you get to work every morning?' – 'Well, usually I go by car.'

3 'Are you .... on the new project?' – 'Yes, I am in charge of the budget.'

4 'He's .... for Brussels on Tuesday.' – 'Oh, then he'll be away for the meeting.'

5 '...................... you like to visit our offices?' – 'No, thanks. I don't have the time.'

6 'He didn't go to the training course.' – 'Well, he should have as he still .... know how the system works.'

7 'The phone is ringing.' – 'Don't worry. I .... get it.'

8 'She's been .... for the company for the last four years.' – 'I didn't know she had been here that long.'

9 'Have you .... given a presentation before?' – 'No. This is the first time.'

10 'If the sales .... improve soon, we'll be in trouble.' – 'Yes. But I'm sure they will.'

11 'Is it OK if I smoke here?' – 'No, I'm afraid you ....'

12 'Apparently they .... us to deliver their order before next Tuesday.' – 'Well, that won't be easy.'

13 'What .... he been doing for the last few days?' – 'I have no idea.'

14 '...................... he really intend to resign next month?' – 'Well, that's what he said.'

15 'What .... you do if you lost your job?' – 'I think I could find another one quite easily.'

16 'Do you think we .... finish this on time?' – 'No way.'

17 'How .... will it take to get there?' – 'We should be there by twelve.'

18 '...................... does she report to?' – 'Her line manager.'

19 '...................... department does he work in?' – 'Sales.'

20 '...................... you agree with what she said?' – 'Yes, I think she was absolutely right.'

21 'We're not .... in buying any of their products.' – 'I know what you mean. They really are too expensive.'

22 '...................... he joined the company there have been a lot of changes.' – 'Yeah. But not all of them have been improvements.'

23 '...................... fault was it?' – 'Actually it was mine. I mixed up the addresses.'

24 'Of the two options, ... one do you prefer?' – 'I think the first one is the best.'

25 '...................... the situation has improved, there are still some problems.' – 'I'm sure we'll be able to sort them out in no time.'

26 '...................... of all we should prepare a plan of action.' – 'Right. Then we can decide what skills we need.'

27 'Orders for the month are down and as a .... we have had to slow down production.' – 'But I'm sure things will pick up soon.'

28 'The company specialises in measurement systems. .... produces machines for all types of testing.' — 'They provide the software, too.'

29 'Before .... the contract you should get it checked by a lawyer.' — 'We've already arranged for someone to have a look at it.'

30 '...................... much would it cost us to rent a new machine?' — 'It could work out at under two thousand pounds a year.'

31 'Can we meet next Monday?' — 'No. I'm afraid I .... be around then.'

32 'Six thousand dollars is far .... expensive for us.' — 'Well, couldn't we ask them for a discount?'

33 'Our products are as .... as any that you can find on the market.' — 'I would say they're actually better than most.'

34 'Did they say how long it would take?' — 'Yes. It's going to be much longer .... we expected.'

35 'Are .... companies working in the same sector?' — 'Yes, but one is more experienced than the other.'

36 'What .... happen if we cancelled our order?' — 'Well, you'd lose your deposit.'

37 'They showed us several different designs.' — 'I really liked the .... that had the green logo on it.'

38 'How .... do you check your e-mail?' — 'I usually look at it first thing in the morning.'

39 'Which of the candidates did you prefer?' — 'To tell you truth, I didn't like .... of them.'

40 '...................... extra clause has been added to the contract.' — 'Oh really? What does it say?'

41 'Fortunately, orders .... across the board last month.' — 'Yes. But it wasn't by very much, was it?'

42 'The documents .... filed alphabetically.' — 'I know that but in which folder are they kept?'

43 '...................... results of the survey will be published next week.' — 'Oh, I can't wait to see them.'

44 'How long have you known about this?' — 'I first heard about it two weeks ....'

45 'If they hadn't wasted so much time, they would .... finished by now.' — 'Well, it's easy to say that.'

46 'Haven't you finished reading that report ....?' — 'No, I'm afraid I haven't even opened it.'

47 'He .... has experience of working in Africa.' — 'I know, that's why we're giving him the job.'

48 'In some cases we are prepared to make exceptions.' — '...................... as?'

49 'The new brochure really is very poor.' — 'Yes. It's definitely the .... one we've produced so far.'

50 'Have you seen their rep recently?' — 'Yeah. He was here .... week.'

Vocabulary

2 (30 points)

One word is missing from each of the following sentences. Write the missing word in the gap. Compounds count as one word. The first letter is given to help you.

1 People who buy shares in a company are called s....................... .

2 Companies protect the copyright of their products and ideas through p....................... .

3 A company owned by another company is a s....................... .

4 When applying for a job you send a CV and a letter of a....................... .

5 Companies which specialise in recruitment are called h....................... .

6 People who apply for jobs are referred to as a....................... .

7 A choice of products may also be called a r....................... of products.

8 Shops and stores are also referred to as retail o....................... .

9 Large food retailers in out-of-town locations are known as s....................... .

10 When a company sells the right to operate a business using its established system or format to another one this is called a f....................... .

11 A booking may also be called a r....................... .

12 Managers d....................... by giving responsibility to people working in their department.

13 The amount of responsibility depends on the position a staff member holds in the h....................... .

14 Charges for professional services are also called f....................... .

15 Banks have many offices or b....................... in different areas or towns.

16 M....................... banks do not deal with the public but with companies.

17 C....................... is the money used by a particular country.

18 To e....................... employees means to give them a greater say in decision-making.

19 R....................... products are made from materials that have already been used.

20 On the stock market you can buy b....................... which are loans to a company or governments.

21 To i....................... shares means to make available to investors units of a company's capital on the stock market.

22 A t....................... is a tax imposed on imported goods.

23 A b....................... is a shipping document which proves ownership or receipt of goods.

24 In accounting, everything a company owns is referred to as its a....................... .

25 A company's l....................... are everything it owes.

26 A statement of e....................... shows how much revenue a company brings into a business.

27 A private company in the US is referred to by the abbreviation l....................... .

28 When two companies come together to form one company, it is known as a m....................... .

29 The process of buying goods and services using the Internet is called e-....................... .

30 P....................... is the term used for a company's offices and buildings.

Total score ______

Mid-course Test

Comprehension

1 (10 Points – 2 points for each correct answer)

Read the following text carefully and answer the questions on page 91.

Tips for Future Franchisees

Have you ever thought of buying your own franchise business?

Before you take the plunge here are a few things to think about:

a Are you the right person to run a franchise?

To be successful in this game you must have the right personality type. This means that you should be the sort of person who can handle the pressures of working long hours, of taking financial risks and of having to deal with all the everyday management problems of running your own business. You will be working in a competitive environment where achievement will be the only guarantee of success. However, stamina and managerial skills are not the only requirements, you must be the kind of person who can accept help and guidance from the franchisor. The franchisee must be willing to comply with the rules and guidelines which are part of an established franchise. If you don't like restrictions and resent being told what to do, then franchising is possibly not the best type of business for you.

b Do you have the necessary business skills?

Managing a franchise involves a combination of different business skills ranging from personnel management to accountancy and business administration. Exactly how much of your time will be spent on each of these aspects of running a business depends on the type of franchise that you decide to open. If you are running a fast food outlet, then hiring and keeping staff will probably take up much of your time. However, if you choose a service franchise you'll probably have to concentrate more on selling yourself to new customers and maintaining good relationships with your existing clients.

c Have you got the financial resources?

You can't start a franchise without money so the first thing to know is how much you can afford to put into the business. This may mean that you will have to mortgage your home and use any personal savings that you may have. But even that may not be enough. You are almost certainly going to need a bank loan to get the business started. Sometimes it may be possible to get financial help from government small business assistance schemes but, if not, you're going to have to work this out with a banker.

d Have you done the background research?

It is essential that you know what you are letting yourself in for. A little research will tell you about the history of the franchise, what the track record is and what problems have arisen in the past. It is also a good idea to carry out some market research to make sure there is a niche for the franchise product or service in your area. If you opt for a retail business, you should be aware of the importance of a good location; Most franchisors will want to inspect the proposed outlet before signing a franchise agreement.

e Which franchise should you choose?

Many people thinking of becoming franchisees see it as the simplest way to start a business. They dream of being their own boss and running their own company but few understand the importance of choosing the right type of franchise. You must believe in the product or service you are going to sell. This will help to establish trust and a good working relationship with the franchisor as well as ensuring a continued dynamic and positive attitude towards the business even if times get tough.

Tick (✓) the correct answer **A**, **B**, or **C** for 1–5 below.

1 According to the text, which of the following personality types would be least likely to succeed in the franchise business:
A an energetic self starter
B a very creative and innovative manager
C an enterprising risk-taker

2 Which of the following points is not implied in paragraph **b**:
A It is very important to organise your time well.
B Many skills are needed to run a franchise business successfully.
C It is difficult to get good staff for fast food outlets.

3 Paragraph **c** stresses which of the following points:
A It is impossible to start a franchise without government assistance.
B Many financial sacrifices may have to be made.
C The bank manager will work out all the finances for the franchisee.

4 According to paragraph **d** research will not:
A inform franchisees of the potential minefields.
B help them choose the right franchise.
C ensure an agreement between the franchisee and franchisor.

5 The main point of paragraph **e** is:
A Franchising is the easiest option when starting a business.
B Running a franchise is very difficult.
C It is essential to like the product or service your're selling.

Vocabulary

2 (30 points – 2 points for each correct answer)

Fill in the blanks with one of the words or phrases from the list below. There are more words than blanks. Change the forms of the words where necessary.

overhead suppliers profits paperwork payroll to tackle lucrative niche regulator shareholder dividend broker to promote to hire authority hierarchy surplus to recycle patent chain executives

1 Our company has over 1000 employees on its ....

2 .... are necessary to ensure fair trading on the stock exchange.

3 The company's ...., including rent, electricity and heating, have doubled this year.

4 The mobile phone market is an extremely .... one.

5 Our .... have never made a late delivery.

6 .... are paid according to company earnings.

7 The company has a lot of financial problems .... before considering expansion.

8 We are going to open a .... of supermarkets in France.

9 Our innovations are protected by ....

10 In most companies major decisions are made high up the ....

11 We're expanding and personnel is presently .... new staff.

12 Who gave you the .... to sign this invoice?

13 Let's sell off our .... stock cheaply in the January sales.

14 Keeping two sets of receipts will involve a lot of extra ....

15 My .... advises me on which shares to buy.

Grammar

3 (20 points)

Put the following verbs into the correct tense.

We .... (**1** to found) the company in 1998 and ever since it .... (**2** to make) money. At present we .... (**3** to expand) our range of products and as always, this .... (**4** to mean) big investments in research and marketing. Recently we .... (**5** to negotiate) a loan with our bank and they .... (**6** to agree) to give us a reasonable interest rate. If the bank .... (**7** not to accept), we .... (**8** to have to) postpone our plans to expand our product line. If everything .... (**9** to go) according to plan, we .... (**10** to launch) the first new item as early as next March. We are happy about this as some of our old products .... (**11** not to sell) as well in recent years so they .... (**12** to replace) by the new, improved ones as soon as possible.

The last few months .... (**13** to be) difficult for the people in our research and development department who .... (**14** to work) an average of ten hours a day and they now .... (**15** to need) a break. The marketing people are also complaining about the lack of staff and if we .... (**16** to have) more money, we .... (**17** to employ) more people. However, decisions about taking on more staff .... (**18** to make) after careful and long consideration. For the moment we .... (**19** to feel) that we .... (**20** not to be) in a financial position to do so.

4 (20 points – 2 points for each correct answer)

Tick (✓) the word or phrase **A**, **B**, **C** or **D** that best completes each sentence.

1 Several customers have phoned us to .... complaints about the quality of our after sales service.
A do **B** make **C** say **D** state

2 .... prices of some goods have risen, this has not affected our overall performance.
A Despite **B** In spite of **C** Although **D** Never mind

3 I hate .... business over the phone.
A doing **B** making **C** do **D** telling

4 She isn't used to .... with such important contracts.
A dealing **B** deal **C** handle **D** negotiate

5 Are you .... working for the same company?
A yet **B** already **C** still **D** always

6 Interest rates have been .... since the government changed.
A rise **B** drop **C** declined **D** falling

7 We never .... to work on Saturdays before this year.
A were used **B** used **C** use **D** are used

8 A lot of progress has been .... in developing new ultra-light materials.
A done **B** did **C** make **D** made

9 The recent devaluation of the currency will result .... many companies going bankrupt.
A from **B** for **C** to **D** in

10 Consumers have shown a marked .... for environmentally packaged goods.
A preferential **B** preferred **C** preference **D** preferring

Total score _____

Final Test

Comprehension

1 (10 Points – 2 points for each correct answer)

Read the following text carefully and answer the questions that follow it.

Today advertisers are having to find innovative ways to attract the attention of increasingly disinterested consumers. Research has shown that although some people consider advertising to be an intrusion into their private lives others, particularly the younger generation, actually enjoy being the target of commercial messages and the more surprising they are the better.

Traditionally advertising has relied on such media as television and magazines to appeal to a broad audience with no guarantee of reaching its target. With increasing competition and more sophisticated market data, companies are now trying to find ways of directly confronting only the specific groups of consumers that interest them.

This has led to an increase in point-of-sale and outdoor advertising which is now taking some new and unexpected forms. For instance, in some supermarkets, food products, such as fruit, carry small stickers advertising totally unrelated products. Similarly, floors in shops, schools and stations have become just another surface on which to place a message – the idea being that you can't get much closer to the customer than under his or her feet.

Visitors to new cities who rent cars are often surprised when they switch on the cassette player to hear commercials for shops, restaurants and interesting places to visit. Cash distributors with talking ads are not uncommon in the US and screens and speakers at petrol pumps, advertising products you can find in neighbouring shops have proven to be very successful in some American cities.

Direct appeal, like this, doesn't only make good marketing sense but it often works out to be less expensive too. Global companies who continue to use the costly broadcast media are also beginning to experiment with ways to guarantee consumer attention by running original and sometimes even shocking adverts where you would normally least expect them. Hardly surprising when you know that the average person will spend several minutes reading your advert every time they go to the washroom. But it is a risky business and these kinds of ads can sometimes backfire. While interest is ensured, the drawback is that some people will be turned off.

So where will it all end? So far, environmentalist groups have managed to stop the promoters of 'space marketing' but one US company still has plans to send giant billboards into orbit that will be big enough for the whole world to see. Get ready for the advertising future where, wherever you look, up or down, someone will be trying to get you to part with your money.

According to the text, are the following true or false? Tick (✓) the right answer.

1 Consumers in general are disinterested in advertising.
True **False**

2 The new methods of advertising are more expensive than the traditional ones.
True **False**

3 TV commercials are a good way to reach a precise target.
True **False**

4 Environmentalists are opposed to marketing in space.
True **False**

5 Some food products carry stickers advertising other types of goods.
True **False**

Vocabulary

2 (30 points – 2 points for each correct answer)

Fill in the gaps with one of the words or phrases from the list below. Change the forms of the words where necessary. There are more words than gaps.

quota	**tariff**	**subsidiary**	**joint venture**	**revenue**	**profit and loss account**
entrepreneurs	**balance sheet**	**brand image**	**merge**	**clash**	**cutting edge**
sole traders	**to monitor**	**slogan**	**invoice**	**licence**	
losses	**auditor**	**imperatives**	**rival**	**hurdles**	

1 We have decided to open a new company by setting up a .... with another company in the same line of business as us.

2 When we want to know what our company is worth at any given dates we consult our ....

3 Our .... are worried about our growing market share.

4 We have asked the shippers to send us their .... as proof that the goods were sent.

5 The .... is checking our accounts for mistakes.

6 The new advertising campaign fits our .... perfectly.

7 We .... with one of our rivals and we now form the biggest software company in the country.

8 Once we get over the initial bureaucratic ...., everything will be fine.

9 When negotiating the agreement we must consider the .... of the shareholders.

10 Our sales have increased thanks to our catchy ....

11 The .... shows how much the company is earning through sales as well as the costs and expenses incurred through sales.

12 .... are inevitable between people with strong personalities.

13 We are setting up a .... of the company in Spain, as part of our expansion programme.

14 With fully computerised production we are at the .... of technology..

15 They are making our products under ....

Grammar

3 (20 points)

Put the following verbs into the correct tense.

Currently, European CEOs .... (**1** to wonder) if mergers are the best way to make deals. While in Japan, mergers .... (**2** to change) the way business works. Last year several European companies .... (**3** to announce) marriages and later called them off, for example; Hoechst, a German group and its French counterpart Rhone-Poulenc, ... (**4** to force) to change the terms of their life-science merger. More recently, however, in Japan, several successful mergers .... (**5** to complete) between national pharmaceutical giants, banks and telecom companies.

Today, Japanese companies .... (**6** to form) alliances with foreign companies, too. But these are early days and nobody knows how long the trend .... (**7** to continue). If the Renault Nissan deal .... (**8** not to be) signed, other Japanese corporations .... (**9** not to consider) foreign or gaijin companies as possible partners. It now seems very likely that we .... (**10** to see) more deals of its kind in the next few years.

Meanwhile, legal and regulatory barriers .... (**11** to be removed) to facilitate negotiations, and in the future minority shareholders .... (**12** to have to) sell their stakes to the acquiring firm once the majority .... (**13** to agree) to a deal. At the moment, shareholders .... (**14** to be able to) refuse to sell if they .... (**15** not to agree).

However, in recent years the biggest obstacle for European mergers .... (**16** not to be) shareholders but the problem of personality clashes between CEOs. If Japanese managers .... (**17** to learn) anything from European managers' mistakes, they .... (**18** to know) that major compromises .... (**19** have to make). Optimistic analysts .... (**20** to look forward to) many successful merger deals in Japan in the near future.

4 (10 points – 2 points for each correct answer)

Tick (✓) the word or phrase **A**, **B**, **C** or **D** that correctly summarises the meaning of the sentence.

1 'I'm afraid we can't give you a bank loan,' said the bank manager. The bank manager said:
- **A** I was afraid I couldn't give you a loan;
- **B** He was afraid he couldn't give me a loan.
- **C** He was afraid he can't give me a loan.
- **D** I'm afraid I couldn't give me a loan.

2 'How long have you been working on this project?' Ms Jenkins asked.
- **A** She asked me if I was working on the project for long.
- **B** She wanted to know if I was working on the project.
- **C** She asked me how long I worked on the project.
- **D** She asked me how long I had been working on the project.

3 'Could you tell him to ring me back as soon as he gets in?' the caller said.
- **A** The caller asked me to get him to ring back.
- **B** It was asked that I ring her back.
- **C** The caller asked me to tell him to ring her back when he got in.
- **D** The caller wanted me to ring back.

4 'We recently acquired a South American distributor,' the company spokesperson said.
A The spokesperson announced that there had been a recent acquisition.
B The spokesperson told that a South American distributor was recently taken over.
C The spokesperson said that they would have acquired a new operation.
D The spokesperson revealed that a company was going to be acquired.

5 'Why don't we postpone the meeting until next week?' the chairman said.
A The chairman suggested that the meeting had been postponed.
B The chairman announced that the meeting would take place next week.
C The chairman said they wanted the meeting postponed.
D The chairman proposed that they postpone the meeting.

Grammar

5 (10 points)

Tick (✓) the word or phrase **A**, **B**, **C** or **D** that best completes each sentence.

1 Since export regulations have been relaxed it has become .... to work in the Indian market.
A more easy **B** more easier **C** difficult **D** easier

2 The new promotional campaign has succeeded .... our product known to a wider audience.
A to make **B** to making **C** for to make **D** in making

3 When you apply for a visa you .... expect to receive it within two weeks.
A don't have to **B** shouldn't **C** needn't **D** could

4 If you travel within the European union you .... carry a passport, as an identity card is sufficient.
A mustn't **B** have to **C** need to **D** don't have to

5 .... the latest information about our products is now possible directly from our web page.
A Obtaining **B** To obtain **C** To obtaining **D** For to obtain

6 The latest series of advertisements are much .... the original ones.
A appealing than **B** as appealing as **C** more appealing than **D** most appealing as

7 Although they finally decided to open the new office in Amsterdam, they .... any other major European city.
A could choose **B** could have chosen **C** could be chosen **D** chose

8 Significant improvements in productivity have resulted .... the introduction of the new order processing software.
A in **B** from **C** into **D** about

9 An organisation .... ours needs to develop new markets in order to survive.
A as **B** like **C** look like **D** unlike

10 Janet Henderson is the person who looks .... all our contracts with foreign suppliers.
A for **B** on **C** after **D** up

Total score ______

Key to photocopiable materials

Key vocabulary exercises

(pp.66–73)

Unit 1
1 Board of Directors
2 Chairperson
3 Managing Director
4 senior managers

Unit 2
1 recruit
2 position
3 apply for
4 letter of application
5 covering letter
6 CV
7 application form
8 shortlist
9 applicants
10 interview
11 hire
12 recruitment agency

Unit 3
1 Retailing
2 shops
3 outlets
4 retail chains
5 multiple retailers
6 shopping centres
7 superstores
8 Department stores

Unit 4
1 franchisor
2 franchisee
3 format
4 franchise agreement
5 franchise fee
6 management services fee
7 advertising fee
8 operations manual
9 master franchisee

Unit 5
1 hierarchy
2 subordinates
3 authority
4 delegate
5 national culture

Unit 6
1 the Bank of England
2 commercial banks
3 clearing banks
4 branches
5 Merchant banks

Unit 7
1 consumer society
2 environment
3 packaging
4 recycled
5 Pollution

Unit 8
1 stock market or stock exchange
2 issue shares
3 institutional investors
4 equities
5 ordinary or common shares
6 broker
7 shareholder
8 stake
9 dividends
10 bonds
11 Securities
12 traded

Unit 9
1 export
2 import
3 tariff
4 quota
5 protectionist

Unit 10
1 markets
2 data
3 financial accounts
4 revenue
5 costs
6 profits
7 losses
8 annual report

Unit 11
1 c
2 a
3 b

Unit 12
1 c
2 a
3 b

Unit 13
1 Marketing
2 product
3 price
4 place
5 promote
6 the four Ps

Unit 14
1 Product advertising
2 to target
3 media
4 Corporate advertising
5 image
6 Public relations
7 publicity

Unit 15
1 media
2 data
3 news
4 print media
5 press
6 channels or stations
7 broadcasts
8 multimedia
9 audiences
10 networks

Diagnostic Test

(p.92–94)

Grammar

1 (50 Points)
1 been
2 do
3 working
4 leaving
5 Would
6 doesn't
7 'll
8 working
9 ever
10 don't
11 can't
12 want / need (also asked / told)
13 has
14 Does
15 would
16 will / can
17 long
18 Who
19 Which
20 Do
21 interested
22 Since
23 Whose
24 which
25 Although / Though
26 First
27 result / consequence
28 It
29 signing
30 How
31 won't / shan't
32 too
33 good
34 than
35 both
36 would
37 one
38 often / regularly
39 any / either
40 An
41 increased
42 are
43 The
44 ago

45 have
46 yet
47 already
48 Such
49 worst
50 last

Vocabulary

2 (30 points)

1 shareholders
2 patents
3 subsidiary
4 application
5 headhunters
6 applicants
7 range
8 outlets
9 superstores
10 franchise
11 reservation
12 delegate
13 hierarchy
14 fees
15 branches
16 Merchant
17 Currency
18 empower
19 Recycled
20 bonds
21 issue
22 tariff
23 bill of lading
24 assets
25 liabilities
26 earnings
27 Inc.
28 merger
29 e-commerce
30 premises

Mid-course Test

(p.95–97)

Comprehension

1 (10 Points – 2 points for each correct answer)

1 B
2 A
3 B
4 C
5 C

Vocabulary

2 (30 points – 2 points for each correct answer)

1 payroll
2 Regulators
3 overheads
4 lucrative
5 suppliers
6 Dividends
7 to tackle
8 chain
9 patents
10 hierarchy
11 hiring
12 authority
13 surplus
14 paperwork
15 broker

Grammar

3 (20 points)

1 founded (past simple)
2 has been making (present perfect)
3 are expanding (present continuous)
4 means (present simple)
5 negotiated (past simple) or have negotiated (present perfect)
6 agreed (past simple) or have agreed (present perfect)
7 had not accepted (third conditional)
8 would have had to (third conditional)
9 goes (first conditional)
10 will launch (first conditional)
11 have not been selling (present perfect continuous)
12 will be replaced (passive)
13 have been (present perfect)
14 have been working (present perfect) or have worked (present perfect)
15 need (present simple)
16 had (second conditional)
17 would employ (second conditional)
18 are made (passive) or will be made (future passive)
19 feel (present simple)
20 are not (present simple)

4 (20 points – 2 points for each correct answer)

1 B
2 C
3 A
4 A
5 C
6 D
7 B
8 D
9 D
10 C

Final Test

(p.98–101)

Comprehension

1 (10 Points – 2 points for each correct answer)

1 True
2 False
3 False
4 True
5 True

Vocabulary

2 (30 Points – 2 points for each correct answer)

1 joint venture
2 balance sheet
3 rivals
4 invoice
5 auditor
6 brand image
7 merged
8 hurdles
9 imperatives
10 slogan
11 profit and loss account
12 Clashes
13 subsidiary
14 cutting edge
15 licence

Grammar

3 (20 points)

1 are wondering (present continuous)
2 are changing (present continuous)
3 announced (past simple)
4 were forced (passive)
5 have been completed (passive)
6 are forming (present continuous)
7 is going to continue / will continue (future)
8 had not been (third conditional)
9 would not have considered (third conditional)
10 will see / are going to see (future)
11 are being removed (passive)
12 will have to (future)
13 agree (present simple)
14 can (modal verb)
15 do not agree (present)
16 has not been (present perfect)
17 learn (first conditional)
18 will know (first conditional)
19 will have to be made (passive)
20 are looking forward to (present continuous as a future tense)

4 (10 points – 2 points for each correct answer)

1 B
2 D
3 C
4 A
5 D

5 (10 points)

1 D
2 D
3 C
4 D
5 A
6 C
7 B
8 A
9 B
10 C

Pearson Education Limited
Edinburgh Gate
Harlow
Essex CM20 2JE
England
and Associated Companies throughout the World
www.longman-elt.com

First published in 2000
Second impression 2000

Set in ITC Stone Serif and ITC Stone Sans

Printed in Spain by Gráficas Estella, S.A.

ISBN 0 582 335566

Designed by Kevin McGeoghegan